The Homesteader's

NATURAL CHICKEN KEEPING

HANDBOOK

The Homesteader's

NATURAL CHICKEN KEEPING

HANDBOOK

RAISING A HEALTHY FLOCK FROM START TO FINISH

Amy K. Fewell

Foreword by Joel Salatin

LYONS PRESS

**GUILFORD,
CONNECTICUT**

An imprint of The Rowman & Littlefield Publishing Group, Inc.
4501 Forbes Blvd., Ste. 200
Lanham, MD 20706
www.rowman.com

Distributed by NATIONAL BOOK NETWORK

British Library Cataloguing in Publication Information available

Library of Congress Cataloging-in-Publication Data available

ISBN 978-1-4930-3739-1 (paperback)
ISBN 978-1-4930-3740-7 (e-book)

♾™ The paper used in this publication meets the minimum requirements of American National Standard for Information Sciences—Permanence of Paper for Printed Library Materials, ANSI/NISO Z39.48-1992.

Printed in the United States of America

To all the crazy chicken keepers: may your egg yolks always be golden,
and your chicken addiction strong.

CONTENTS

Foreword by Joel Salatin

"Can I hold one?" Although not grammatically correct (it should be "*May* I hold one?"), this is by far and away the most common first response to any child's first encounter with chickens on our farm. Unlike factory farms, we encourage visitors and do all we can to facilitate an up-close and personal encounter with our feathered friends.

Of course, I always oblige, whether it's a new fluffy chick or a softly feathered adult. Holding an animal that actually feeds us, that sustains our lives, is truly magic. That more people today have never had such a visceral encounter is a deficiency I aim to rectify. Unlike a cow or horse, chickens are small enough to be cuddled by even little children. And they aren't dogs or cats, which puts them in a unique relational category.

Nearly half a century ago, as a teenager, I had two pet Rhode Island Red chickens. Named Big Red and Little Red, these two, unlike the others in my several-hundred-bird commercial egg-laying flock, had managed to escape their shelters and turned rogue. Perhaps that's what won my heart. As a budding innovative entrepreneur, I couldn't help but respect and endorse their free-range prowess. With timely sleuthing I found where these two independent-minded ladies were laying their eggs, which protected me from lost production.

I have numerous pictures of them perched on my head and other poses that anyone would assume among friends. They never asked for food, living many years scavenging things around the barnyard. For the chicken-uninitiated, superlatives to describe hen resourcefulness are an exercise in futility. They eat mice, fly larvae, weeds, grasshoppers. Goodness, a better farmstead sanitizer would be hard to imagine.

When folks ask me how to feed their blossoming interest in all things regenerative, my standard answer is "kitchen chickens." And yes, that includes an apartment or condominium. Throw out the gerbil and snake, the cockatoo and the aquarium. In the same space, keep a couple of chickens. And if you have teenagers, you'll never find a better role model. They rise, eagerly and happily, at dawn's first light, spend all day converting trash and problems into treasure, and at the first sign of dwindling light, go to bed. Does that not epitomize how teens should behave?

On our farm, nothing performs as many useful roles as pastured poultry. And in the winter, we house them in tall tunnels where they de-bug residual summer vegetables and create beautiful compost for next season's crops. While eggs may not be the most profitable enterprise on our farm, they provide daily cash flow. The old-time "butter 'n' egg" money kept many farmsteads afloat during economic downturns. In today's urbanizing economy, eggs are the gateway product to other things. Nothing drives sales and marketing like a tasty, nutritious egg.

I'll never forget a Coast Guard service member who seemed to be fighting a losing battle with high cholesterol. I told him about my wife Teresa's grandmother, who at 90 years old was fighting the same battle. We took her a dozen pickled eggs; she ate six of them in one day and had blood work done the next morning. She had forgotten about the routine doctor's appointment. For the first time in a decade, her numbers were good. After relaying this anecdote to the middle-aged Coast Guard visitor in our sales building, I sold him several dozens of eggs. The next week, after eating half a dozen a day for several days, he went in for a routine annual medical exam and for the first time in a decade had normal numbers. I know because he wrote me a letter about it.

Growing or acquiring food that powerful should be the goal of every conscientious person, don't you think? Where do eggs like this come from? They certainly don't come from factories. They can't be concocted Star Trek–style in a laboratory. They come from the humble utilitarian hen treated to a habitat that allows her to fully express her chicken-ness.

I always thought the chickens at our Polyface Farm received royal treatment. But after reading *The Homesteader's Natural Chicken Keeping Handbook*, I think if I were a reincarnationist, I'd want to be a chicken in Amy Fewell's flock. Of course, smaller flocks lend themselves to more individual attention. But that's the point. World-class eggs require world-class care. And world-class anything earns that vaunted position because it's special.

I have never seen such an eclectic blend of health and curative directives, from a nonchemical approach, as Amy has assembled in these pages. When you raise as many thousands of chickens as we do on our farm, seeing the individual needs and treating ailments often doesn't make economic sense. Amy's attention and ability to treat her chickens like I would a family dairy cow is both inspiring and convicting.

On our farm, we've had three sickness issues over the half century we've been raising chickens. The first was a nutritional weakness in the ration, rectified by using a good organic premix supplement called Nutri-Balancer. The second was a crowded housing situation due to extremely cold, wet outside conditions in early spring that delayed our chickens from going out to pasture. Birds can grow a lot in two weeks, and by the time the weather cleared, this particular flock was highly stressed. The third time occurred with an associate who was growing some turkeys for us and, unbeknownst to us, not doing a good job. The extremely unsanitary conditions brought stress, which brought on respiratory problems that took us a couple of years to finally eradicate.

The common denominator in all three of these situations? My fault. That is a common thread in this wonderful book from Amy. Yes, chickens can get sick, but usually it's because of a management snafu. Providing a good habitat and offering the best immune-building care possible is the best way to ensure a pleasant poultry experience. Given the right care, chickens are quite hardy in the main. Fortunately, the inevitable loss of one is not as economically devastating as losing a cow or horse.

For anyone intimidated by the thought of being responsible for a couple of chickens, this handbook will coach you into success. And for people like me, this offers more options to make sure the whole flock reaches its full potential. After we've done well, we can always do better. This highly readable, practical book has something for chicken enthusiasts no matter what the scale. If you've never felt comfortable enough to actually get a couple of backyard chickens, please start. It will add new dimensions to your life. If you already have some chickens but wish they could thrive better, here is your ticket to success.

If you've ever wondered what happens when an herbalist meets a flock of chickens, here is your answer. In the world of farmstead flockstering, nobody sets the bar higher than Amy. We could all aspire to this level of care. Read and enjoy.

Introduction

It happened one afternoon while we were driving home from town. I was sitting in the passenger seat of our vehicle, minding my own business, when my husband Mark said, "You know, we should get some chickens." I quickly turned to look at him, confused and surprised. His eyes were still on the road as if he'd never uttered a word. I could tell he was in deep thought. *Did he really just say that?* I chuckled a bit and said, "Yeah, right," but was abruptly met with his reasoning as to why we should get chickens for our backyard.

I didn't realize how serious he was until I found myself, along with my toddler and husband, in the middle of an aisle at our local hardware store purchasing plywood and lumber for our new 8-by-8-foot chicken coop. *Oh, I guess he really was serious!*

As if that wasn't enough proof, a friend of mine had heard we were wanting chickens and said she had left two laying hens wandering her farm when they moved to Texas just one week prior. Apparently we were being gifted two chickens that we had to search high and low for in the middle of a Virginia field on an extremely warm autumn evening. *We hadn't even built the coop yet!*

Now, if you know anything about my husband, you know that his patience can be extremely short. Looking back on this excursion, I wish I would've recorded the happenings of that evening, because no one ever believes me when I tell them that he spent over an hour trying to catch two chickens for a chicken coop we hadn't even built yet. The flailing arms, the "here, chicky chicky," the wings in our faces because the chickens rebelled and refused to be taken away from their freedom.

Finally, we caught them.

We simultaneously threw ourselves into the front seat of our vehicle, sweat pouring off of us, feathers in our hair, mud on our boots, faces caked with dusty Virginia dirt . . . and chickens in a crate in the backseat with our toddler. We looked back at them, looked at each other, and laughed until we couldn't laugh anymore.

As we drove away from that farm, we had no idea what was in store for us, or what the future would hold for us as new chicken keepers—excitement, heartache, stress, happiness, pain, inconvenience, joy. We went from standardized farming practices in the beginning to now using completely holistic approaches with herbs and other natural ways of chicken care. Not only have chickens taught me how to be natural in my chicken keeping practices, but they've also taught me how to organically involve my family as well.

Our chicken journey may have begun on a whim, but chickens truly were the gateway animal for our homestead. With a dream of living a more sustainable lifestyle, growing our own food, and getting back to the land, chickens have been one of the biggest steps we've taken to accomplish part of that self-sustaining lifestyle dream. And believe it or not, they are one of the easiest livestock animals to care for, no matter where you live.

Chicken keeping in and of itself can be practiced two different ways—conventionally or holistically. It can also be a hodgepodge of both, as you'll find in this book. Both of them will make a great impact on the health of your chickens, your homestead, and your own body. The real question is, which way is the healthiest way for you, your chickens, and your family?

We've tried them both; we've tried it all. But after years of chicken keeping we've found the greatest success is holistic care for all of our livestock and within our own family. We are true believers in the "you are what you eat" motto, but we are also believers in being good stewards of the land. If we want to live a holistic lifestyle, shouldn't our chickens live one as well?

There are so many stories I could tell you about our chicken keeping adventures, and I plan to do exactly that throughout this book, from raising rare breeds of chickens and the lice disaster that ensued, to the joy of seeing our first farm-fresh eggs in the little hands of our toddler son. We've been there, done that, got the T-shirt.

I'll share with you some of our own personal experiences, how we do what we do, all while embracing the holistic and natural way of chicken keeping.

There are plenty of books that will tell you all about chickens, but I was never able to find a book that taught me how to raise chickens naturally and holistically throughout *every* stage and *type* of chicken keeping. As an herbalist, when I began applying how I raise my family to the wonderful world of chicken keeping, I was amazed at the outcome. From dark orange, home-raised, omega-3 enriched eggs to the raising of meat birds to the healthiest chickens we've ever had, I'm here to share our chicken keeping basics and trades with you—as an herbalist, a homesteader, and an advocate for free-range chickens and children.

In this book I'll walk you through every stage of chicken keeping and teach you in easy-to-understand terminology with scientific backup. We'll walk through chicken history and breeds, chicken terminology, hatching and brooding, how to properly purchase chickens, basic coop needs, how to care for chickens naturally, how to make your own feed, how to create herbal products, and even how to run a successful egg business and create some amazing recipes from scratch!

The first part of this book was created to be simple and educational for you, but I think you'll find a few sections that romanticize the beautiful world of chicken keeping. Part 4 is an ode to the glorious egg layer. And in Part 6, in true farmhouse style, I'll talk about the beauty of a family that gathers together—whether it's in the chicken coop or around the farmstead table.

My wish is that you'll walk away feeling empowered, encouraged, and inspired to raise your own chickens naturally, by using herbs, a natural diet, a little bit of patience, and a whole lot of joy.

Happy Chicken Keeping!

-Amy

The New Chicken Keeper

SO YOU HAVE A FEW CHICKENS, or you're thinking of getting some, but if you're anything like me, when I first started researching chickens I had no idea how complicated it would be to learn "all the things." Not to mention, it was increasingly hard to find all-natural ways to keep chickens. From the history of the chicken, learning chicken lingo and terminology, all the way to treating your chickens naturally when they get sick—all of the information was, and sometimes still can be, extremely overwhelming.

But it doesn't have to be. For the new chicken keeper, it's easy to become overwhelmed with information overload. *Which breed is better? What's the difference between a pullet and a hen? Why does my chicken have a weird-looking comb?* These are all questions we may ask ourselves at one point or another along our chicken keeping journey.

That's why I've designed the first part of this book to be your guide to "all things chicken," including terms and other important information. After that, we can really start diving into the super-fun parts of chicken keeping!

CHICKEN HISTORY
AND TERMINOLOGY

Chickens have taken over the world! We can find chickens in most suburban backyards, on commercial farms, and even on postage-stamp-size subdivision properties. Chickens are everywhere in the twenty-first century, and rightfully so. From their amazing egg-laying capabilities to their quirky character traits, chickens are one of the most entertaining and beneficial animals on the homestead. But where did the chicken come from? Why are chickens so popular? And how, exactly, did they get here?

The Early History of the Chicken

We know that chickens have been popular for at least the last 7,000 years. In fact, chicken bones were thought to be found at a dig site in northeastern China, dating all the way back to 5,400 BC. Talk about historic! Or prehistoric?

It is thought that the oldest ancestor of the modern chicken is the red junglefowl, from the genus *Gallus* (from which all chickens are descended), which wandered across Asia in 3,000 BC and before. It wasn't just the red junglefowl that is thought to have contributed to today's chickens, though. There are many different subspecies of the junglefowl, including the gray junglefowl from southern India and others stretching across Java, Vietnam, Burma,

and Bangladesh. Junglefowl were everywhere, much like chickens are today. They were a healthy dual-purpose landrace, offering meat and eggs to farmers and homesteaders.

Egyptians enjoyed the self-sufficiency of chickens so much that they created some of the very first incubators in order to hatch more chicken eggs than a mother hen could. By using a series of connected corridors and vents, the incubating chambers were heated by straw, organic material, and livestock (mostly camel) dung.

Centuries of cross-subspecies breeding led to other types of chickens, and just like that, chickens became a sustainable resource for villagers, homesteads, and even empires. Vikings and settlers carried chickens on boats to new lands and along roadways to new settlements. Soldiers carried chickens in crates on wagons and horseback, never knowing how long they'd be gone. It was easier to get an egg from a chicken (or dispatch the chicken itself) as a source of protein than it was to hunt and trap in the midst of battle.

The chicken was more than just a meat and egg source, though. In many cultures and religions, the hen was seen as a symbol of fertility and motherhood. Likewise, the rooster was seen as a symbol of courage and virility.

According to the writings of Roman politician Marcus Tullius Cicero, at the Battle of Drepana in 249 BC the senior flagship magistrate, Publius Clodius Pulcher, practiced the Roman religious requirement of observing chickens before battle. When offered grain, if the chickens fed well on the grain, it meant the battle would be successful because it was blessed by the gods. If the chickens didn't feed well on the grain, the battle would be lost. Unfortunately, Pulcher's chickens didn't eat the grain, and he became so angry that he tossed them overboard. Pulcher lost the battle, leaving almost every single one of his ships at the bottom of the sea. Coincidence?

In the Gospels of the Bible, the rooster was used to fulfill the prophecy of Peter denying Jesus three times "before the cock crows," thus signifying that Peter had denied the Savior of the world. Because of this, in the ninth century, Pope Nicholas I ordered that every church place a rooster on top of its roof or steeple as a reminder of this history. To this day, there are still many churches with rooster weathervanes.

Throughout history, chickens have been a noble and sought-after bird. Even today, chickens continue to make history. Many backyards are dotted with foraging chickens, and commercial egg and meat industries have changed the face of our food system, though not necessarily always for the better.

In 1873 the American Poultry Association (APA) was organized in an effort to maintain a standard of excellence for chicken breeds and to establish a way to classify chicken breeds. This is where many of our chicken breeds originated. Almost everything we know about certain breeds is derived from hours of research and observation from the APA. From comb structure to coloring and more, the APA has helped revolutionize the way we see chickens today.

Chicken History in the United States

Since the late 1800s, we've seen an increase in chickens and their uses in the United States, most likely due to the interest of the APA and other organizations. Here is a brief timeline of chickens in the American household from the 1800s to more modern times.

The 1800s to the early 1900s:

Many households had backyard flocks of dual-purpose birds (birds providing meat and eggs, simultaneously) during this time. Chickens often only laid modestly, about 150 eggs each year. With the exception of a Sunday dinner or special holiday or

My relatives, Edna Hitt and Helen "Mae" Smith Pullen (toddler), late 1940s, taking a photo while tending to chickens.

event meals, chickens weren't consistently raised for meat. They were most often used for their egg production, though eggs could be sparse at times. Vintage homesteaders didn't use supplemental lighting or offer vitamin D supplements in their feed, so chickens were naturally allowed to rest and recuperate during the darker winter months before beginning their egg-laying season once again in the spring.

The 1920s through the 1940s:

The infamous broiler breed of chicken was introduced to communities based in the Delmarva Peninsula area of the United States, as well as Georgia, Arkansas, and New England, in the early 1920s. Many backyard chicken keepers would begin small flocks for their own meat consumption, but most still preferred the easier to find (and manage) dual-purpose breeds.

Mrs. Wilmer Steele was probably one of the first pioneers when it came to the broiler industry. In 1923 you might see her out in the field tending a flock of 500 chicks that she intended to sell as meat to the local community. Just three years later, in 1926, her little side business had become so successful that she built a broiler house that could hold 10,000 broiler birds.

In the 1930s the egg-laying business began to take on a bigger role in society. Some backyard farmers would raise large flocks of chickens, normally about 400 or so. These flocks would free-range about the farm without any confinement. They were housed in large, wide length and narrow width coops with roosting bars and nesting boxes. This looked nothing like the commercial egg industry today. However, with so many chickens, diseases and parasites could often be a problem in flocks. Hens tended to lay only 150 eggs a year, compared to the current 250-plus eggs a year for some modern commercial egg layers.

During this time, my own grandparents and great-grandparents were creating businesses off of their homestead chickens. When my grandmother was a child in the 1930s and '40s, her job was to tend the chickens. They raised bantams specifically to be able to hatch their own eggs, as they are best known for this ability. My grandmother also remembers selling eggs and other farm-fresh goodness to the community. City trucks would often come to the farm, purchase large amounts of fresh harvests (be it eggs, vegetables, meat, or honey), and tote the products to large cities in Virginia to sell to those who didn't live the farming lifestyle.

The 1920s and '30s also brought with it the Great Depression. Chicken keeping wasn't just a want, it was a necessity. Raising self-sufficient breeds and tending to your chickens was an easy source of food and a potential income for those who had chickens. Mountain folk, homesteaders, and farmers across the country (and beyond) could easily tend to this small livestock animal while oftentimes having to get rid of larger livestock, like cattle and pigs, because they were more costly to raise.

Cousin Helen "Mae" Smith Pullen (toddler) and cousin Edna Hitt picking flowers in the field while their flocks range behind them, late 1940s

Other farmers and homesteaders, especially in the "hollers" of West Virginia, didn't have any idea that there was a Great Depression happening. Their homesteading lifestyle had already prepared them to live within their means with easy-to-tend livestock like chickens. So many historic photos show our ancestors on farms, surrounded by chickens and farm equipment. Everyone had chickens, whether they wanted them or needed them.

The 1950s through the 1990s:

In 1949 the United States Department of Agriculture (USDA) launched a voluntary grading program for meat and eggs, and by 1952 the broiler industry officially overtook the regular, everyday chicken farmer. Media and news companies were marketing meat and eggs on a regular basis under name brands by the 1960s and '70s, along with programs that promised disease eradication and stated false claims like "brown eggs are healthier." The chicken business took off, but it took out the vintage farmer and homestead along with it.

In the 1970s, books such as Carla Emery's famous *Encyclopedia of Country Living* opened the floodgates to a new self-sufficiency movement. People were beginning to notice that our food source was changing right before our eyes, and many wanted to get back to living off of the land and, yes, raising chickens. Carla's book inspired many people to take control of their lives again, but the movement didn't last long enough to capture most of my parents' generation.

When the 1980s rolled around, the modern family preferred preprocessed, already cut-up chicken for dinner. The '80s housewife no longer wanted to butcher or buy a whole bird to cut up, and sometimes it was because she didn't have the time, which meant she also didn't have time to worry about chicken keeping. There was a decrease in chicken keeping and a substantial increase in name-brand, preprocessed birds and eggs. The American family now had two parents who worked full-time, children in school, and no time to think about the homesteading lifestyle. Life was busier, and families wanted all the shortcuts they could take.

As a child in the 1990s, I can remember growing up around my grandparents' farm. Believe it or not, they never had chickens when I was little. They don't even have chickens now. They have had cattle for as long as I can remember, even to this day, but even they fell into the ease of prepackaged foods and time constraints. We bought eggs that had a little red "EB" stamp on the tops of them, because we really thought they were the "best." And while home-cooked meals were delicious, they didn't come from the backyard any longer. Honestly, I didn't know any differently.

When my grandmother explained to me as a child that chicks come from chicken eggs, I vowed to never eat eggs again. I was horrified. I literally had no idea that this was a normal part of life because my own family hadn't embraced the homesteading lifestyle that my grandparents grew up in. We were a modern family, a busy family, and getting a chicken would've been more like getting a pet than actually caring about raising a healthy chicken flock to sustain our needs.

Not only had my family lost the skill set of natural chicken keeping, but we had also lost the desire to keep chickens at all.

2000 to the present day:

Now that I'm an adult, I've gotten over the vow I made decades ago to never eat chicken eggs again. There are now chickens freely roaming in my backyard. We process our own excess roosters that we hatch from our own incubator. We have a freezer full of chicken, whether it's from a sustainable farm source or our own flock. Fresh eggs are collected every single day from our large chicken coop, and there's a chocolate cake in the oven made with eggs that were just laid this morning.

At the beginning of the twenty-first century, people began questioning their lifestyles, just as they had in the 1970s. Our food sources were especially in question. In 2001, when Sally Fallon published her book *Nourishing Traditions*, a fire was

ignited in the hearts of so many people who had begun learning about traditional foods and how to raise and prepare them. From the 1920s into the 1960s, Americans watched their food sources become tainted with antibiotics, unnecessary livestock treatments, and false health claims from the industrial food complex. People slowly began gardening and relearning homesteading skills they had almost lost. Even today, people are still becoming more and more aware of the issues in our food system.

However, it wasn't until 2008 that people really began tossing around the idea of having chickens in their backyard once again. Chickens? Really? Could a yuppie in suburbia even take care of chickens without overalls and a straw hat? Many things contributed to modern chicken keeping, including the recession, which caused people to think about raising their own food and where their food came from.

It didn't matter if you had overalls and a straw hat, though, because by 2010 backyard chickens were popping up everywhere. There were chickens in every backyard, whether you lived in the middle of nowhere or in the middle of a sub-division. There were even pet chickens in apartments and on back decks of town-houses. Questions weren't asked—you simply came home with chickens, set up a little chicken coop, and suddenly you became a chicken keeper overnight.

And why not? Chickens are one of the easiest livestock animals to tend for just about any household. What Carla Emery began in the 1970s caught on with my generation in the early 2000s . . . finally!

A New Type of Chicken Keeper

A new type of chicken keeper has been born in the twenty-first century. We're rais-ing chickens because they are fun, because we want to know where our food comes from, because they are easy to raise, because they are sustainable, and because we are

confident that we can actually raise them whether we're farmers or not. We're not just "raising" chickens, though—we're raising chickens *differently*. We're raising chickens *naturally*, with a desire to give them as good a life as we have. Not only are chickens feeding us naturally with their eggs and meat, but we're feeding *them* naturally too, because we know that it makes a difference in our own bodies in the long run.

I know that the chicken keeper within me not only wants to learn new and incredible things about raising chickens naturally, but also wants to share those things with others. And because of this desire in so many of us, we may just change the face of chicken keeping altogether—back to a time when chickens dotted every single pasture and yard because, well, it was just that natural.

General Chicken Keeping Terminology

Whether you're just getting into chickens and you're in the research phase or you're already into chickens and you're wondering what in the world all of this newfound language means, this next section is for you.

When my family first got chickens, I remember mingling in our local online chicken education group. I was seeing all of these new words that made zero sense to me. *How on earth was I going to be a good chicken keeper if I didn't even know the difference between a pullet and a hen?*

What follows is general chicken keeping terminology you'll need to know about the wonderful world of chickens and while reading this book. For more specific terminology (like the different types of chicken combs, breeds, etc.), you'll find those in their appropriate chapters and sections.

Chicks and Hatching

Brooder: the place you house your chicks, with a heat source, until they can be transitioned into the flock.

Broody hen: a hen that chooses to hatch her own eggs.

Broody warning/scream: the loud scream that a broody hen typically emits while nesting; this is completely normal.

Candling: the process of shining light into an egg that has been incubated to check the viability of life.

Chick: a baby chicken.

Clutch: a nest of eggs that a broody hen has decided to hatch.

Incubator: a machine that hatches eggs through heat and air circulation.

Juvenile: a young chicken between the chick and adult chicken stage (typically between 8 and 18 weeks old).

Non-setter: a breed of chicken that does not typically go broody.

Pip (or pipping): the small hole (or act of making the hole) that a chick pokes through the egg when getting ready to hatch.

Straight-run: an unsexed group of chicks, meaning the hatchery has not yet sexed them to be sold either as males or females only.

Zipping: the process that a hatching chick goes through by circling around the egg (inside) and creating a row of holes so that it can pop the top off of the egg to hatch.

General Chicken Terms

Bloom: the protective coating on the eggshell.

Chook: a term for chicken or fowl, used throughout Europe and Australia.

Cock: an adult male chicken.

Cockerel: a juvenile male chicken.

Comb: the top portion of the chicken's head that is (typically) red and fleshy and normally stands upright.

Cull: the act of getting rid of a chicken, either through butchering or selling.

Egg song: the consistent squawk that a hen makes for the first minute after she lays an egg.

Hen: an adult female chicken.

Layer: an adult female chicken that lays eggs consistently.

Molt: the process of shedding old feathers to make room for new ones, typically taking place in late summer or fall.

Pullet: a juvenile female chicken.

Rooster: a male chicken.

Spurs: the large talons that protrude from inside the legs of a male chicken, though some females can have spurs as well.

Vent: the area of a hen where an egg is expelled.

Wattle: the large flaps of flesh that dangle from a chicken's chin.

Chicken Housing

Bedding: the material that lines the coop floors and nesting boxes, typically straw, wood shavings, cardboard chips, or organic matter.

Coop: the dwelling where chickens are safely housed.

Nesting box: the box where a chicken lays her eggs

Roost: the high bars in the chicken coop that chickens perch on at night to sleep.

While there is plenty of other terminology that you can learn, these are some of the top ones you'll use most often. As you dive into the world of breeding, the chicken business, or other chicken adventures, your vocabulary will expand and become much more elaborate.

These terms will mean so much more to you as a chicken keeper as you become more attuned to your chicken flock's needs.

CHAPTER

2

CHICKEN CHARACTERISTICS AND BREEDS

The first two chickens we ever had were a Buff Orpington and a Leghorn. Not necessarily the most exotic pair in the hundreds of chicken breeds, but they served their purpose and we loved them extremely well. Doris, our Buff Orpington, was the fattest hen in the barnyard. Note that I said fattest, not fastest! You could walk outside with a bag of treats and then start running the other way for fear she would run you down. Emily, the Leghorn, was petite and independent. She much more enjoyed wild foraging than sitting on our laps begging for mealworms like Doris did (the girl had no shame, really!).

Both chickens had completely different characteristics, yet both served the same purpose here—to lay eggs for our family table. Let's talk about some of the different characteristics of chickens, both physical and beyond.

Types of Combs

Different breeds have several different characteristics, and one of the first things you'll notice are the different types of combs.

Pea comb. Pea combs are usually three little rows of combs with pea-shaped bumps along the top of them. Sometimes there may

From left to right: (top row) Pea comb, Single comb, Strawberry comb, Cushion Comb, (bottom row) Walnut comb, Buttercup comb, V-shaped comb, and Rose comb.

only be one row of comb. Pea comb birds are great for colder climates because they aren't as susceptible to frostbite.

Single comb. The most common of combs, this comb is just one large straight comb with spikes, starting at the bird's beak and running all the way back to the top of the head.

Strawberry comb. This comb sits fairly flat and sometimes even resembles a strawberry.

Cushion comb. Smaller than a strawberry comb but very similar, this comb is small and flat to the head but creates a little cushion type of comb that sits right between the eyes.

Walnut comb. Much like the cushion comb, the walnut comb is right between the eyes of the chicken and forms a little pillow-like comb. However, walnut combs do have more of a walnut-type shape and can get rather large.

Buttercup comb. This comb has one very small single comb in the middle and two larger combs on either side of the middle comb. The three combs fan out in appearance.

V-shaped comb. This comb is the most interesting. The comb begins fairly flat, and then at the top of the head two thin points come up, creating a comb that looks like two horns.

Rose comb (spiked and non-spiked). Rose combs are very close to the head. Sometimes they are flat, other times they have small nodules on them. At times they may come to a point towards the back end of the head, causing it to be a spiked rose comb.

Types of Feather Patterns

More often than not, you'll see a solid pattern on most of the chickens you keep. This means the bird doesn't have a pattern at all—it is just one solid color. However, there are a few incredible feather patterns you might want to learn about. The most prominent difference between chicken breeds is their feathers and different pattern types.

Barred. Most commonly found with Barred Rock and Crele chickens, the barring pattern is a straight bar of color alternating with a lighter bar of color.

Mottled. Mottled feathering is one of my favorites. These chicken feathers have a light color at the base followed by a dark band of

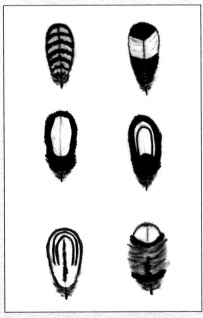

From left to right: (top row) barred, mottled, (middle row) single laced, double laced, (bottom row) penciled, spangles.

coloring and then the chicken's regular standard color. You'll find these feathers on birds like the Mottled Java and Houdan.

Single laced. One of my favorite color patterns, these feathers are outlined with a dark color and then the chicken's standard color. Laced Wyandottes are most commonly known for this trait.

Double laced. Much like the single laced, these feathers are outlined with a dark color, then a similar outline of their standard color, then another dark V-shaped line, and then their standard color again. These are some of the most beautiful feathers you'll see, almost like a chevron pattern. Barnevelders are most commonly known for this feather pattern.

Penciled. Similar to laced feathers, penciled feathers have two distinctive lines in the feathers. However, penciled lines do not outline the entire feather. Instead, two intricate lines contour to the shape without trimming the outside of the feather. Sometimes there can be three or four lines of penciling in each feather. Breeds that display this feather pattern are the Penciled Cochin and Penciled Hamburg.

Feathered or Clean Legs?

I can remember the first time I saw a chicken with feathers on its legs. I thought it was some deformity. So imagine my surprise when I bought a breed that was supposed to have feathers on its legs . . . but it didn't. Yeah, that's another story for the breeding chapter! Most chicken breeds come with clean legs, meaning there are no feathers running down the shaft of their legs. However, other breeds—like Marans and Cochins—have extensive feathering down the shaft of their legs. This is a completely normal characteristic for these breeds.

Spangled. This feather pattern is very similar to the mottled feather pattern, except the loss of pigment occurs in the middle of the feather rather than at the tip. Both ends of the feather have a general color, but the middle of the feather is lighter. Sometimes this can make the feathers look like they have little drops of color on them. The Spangled Hamburg is most commonly known for this pattern.

Egg Colors

Those glorious eggs are what really seal the deal for every chicken keeper. Some folks just want plain white or brown eggs, while others want the more unusual ones—dark chocolate brown, olive green, bright blue, and even pink or purple!

If you're like me, you want every single egg color in your basket. A rainbow of eggs in my vintage egg basket brings me an immense amount of joy.

The color of the egg your chicken lays ultimately depends on the breed and genetics. There are different ways to tell which chicken breeds will lay a certain-colored egg. These methods are not always foolproof, but they certainly do hold some truth to them. I would say these methods work about 75 to 80 percent of the time. But keep in mind that if you want a certain-colored egg, you'll need to purchase that specific breed, rather than just going by these methods.

Ear lobe method. Most of the time, chickens that have white or shiny white or blue earlobes will lay white eggs. Chickens that have red earlobes typically lay brown eggs. *But what about the colored-egg layers?* You see, that's where the exceptions come in. Sometimes colored-egg layers can also have red earlobes, so we'll need a different method to help tell them apart.

Green, blue, or slate-gray legs method. Chickens that have a greenish blue or slate gray tint to their legs often lay colored eggs. This isn't always a tried-and-true method, as mixed breeds

can be hard to decipher. Chickens with slate-gray legs can also lay a pinkish egg.

These two methods are fun to experiment with. Just keep in mind that it's not a foolproof way to discover what color eggs your chicken will lay.

Why Are There Different-Colored Eggs?

The chicken's reproductive system is quite intriguing, and you might be wondering how on earth those eggs become different colors. It's thought that all hens' eggs start out as white in the egg canal, but depending on the breed, as the egg passes through the oviduct of the chicken, minerals are deposited onto the egg. Each breed has a different coloring of these minerals, which causes different colors of eggs.

One of the neatest things I've experienced in chicken keeping is when I've watched some of my colored-egg layers (especially the olive and blue ones) lay a fresh egg, and if I quickly pick it up while it's still slightly wet, the pigment will sometimes end up on my hands. I simply wash it off with a little water or wipe my hands on my jeans.

Who needs dyes when you have naturally dyed Easter eggs straight from the chicken? (We'll talk more about the process of the egg and the chicken's reproductive system in chapter 11.)

Types of Chicken Breeds

Combs and feather patterns are incredibly fun to look at, as are beautiful baskets of colorful eggs, but physical characteristics alone don't "make" the chicken. There are different breeds for different purposes. Some even have multiple purposes, or are what we call "dual-purpose." Before we get into some of the top breeds of chickens, let's walk through each purpose of the bird. The more you understand the purpose, the better you can choose your breeds.

Layers. These breeds were specifically bred for laying eggs, such as Leghorns and hybrid sexlinks. Sexlinks are especially popular egg layers, as they are easy to sex by color at time of birth. We'll talk about this more in the breeds section. Egg-laying breeds offer delicious eggs on a daily basis. They typically have a more slender body type, but don't let that smaller size fool you. They can lay fairly large eggs!

Meat. These chickens are typically bred for meat only. While there are certainly meat breeds, like the Red Ranger, that can also be a dual-purpose bird, meat chickens are generally a hybrid, like the Cornish X. Hybrid meat birds are often processed at 8 weeks of age, and sometimes can't move about very well due to the weight of their quickly growing muscles. However, it is entirely possible to pasture-raise these breeds without distress on their bodies—they just tend to grow a little more slowly.

Dual-purpose. Some of the best homestead breeds are dual-purpose birds. These chickens are bred for their exceptional laying quality and their ability to be used as a meat source. Dual-purpose chickens have broader body types and carry a bit more weight than layers do, but they still tend to be great layers for the family table. In this category you'll find breeds like the Orpington, Jersey Giant, Plymouth Rock, Delaware, and Brahma—to name a few. Many heritage breeds lend themselves well to being dual-purpose birds, while hybrids tend to be better egg layers.

Bantam. These breeds are extremely small chickens, though they act like other chickens when it comes to their big personalities. Some regular breeds even come in a bantam size, like the Plymouth Rock and Ameraucana. Typical bantam breeds are the Serama, Sebright, and Japanese. Bantams generally lay slightly smaller eggs than the average chicken, while some lay much smaller eggs. It takes about two bantam eggs to make one large chicken egg. While they aren't giant-egg layers, they have proven time and time again to be exceptional broody hens and mothers. And the roosters are quite feisty as well!

If you're looking to raise a specific breed, you'll want to know what that breed standard is. Breed standards (physical and temperamental characteristics of the breed) are set by the American Poultry Association and are called the *Standard of Perfection* The Standard of Perfection guide can be ordered online at http://www.amerpoultryassn.com/store.htm.

Heritage, Hybrid, or Landrace?

You're probably thinking, *Wait, you mean there are even* more *types of breeds before we even get to the* actual *breeds?* Sure there are! But this distinction is pretty important and might mean the difference between having just "chickens" and actually having *self-sustaining* chickens.

Heritage breed chickens are birds that have been around for centuries. They have a standard through the APA, and they are generally great dual-purpose birds. When

bought from a reputable breeder, many will even go broody and be a wonderful sustainable breed for you—hatching their own chickens, giving you lots of eggs, and even being a great meat bird.

Hybrid breed chickens are breeds that have been "created," such as the sexlink or Cornish X. They were created for one purpose and one purpose only. Sexlinks were created for the sole purpose of laying eggs, sometimes as many as 320 per year. You get a sexlink by crossing two heritage breeds, therefore creating a sexlink breed of offspring. Sexlinks are easy to sex at hatching because the males and females have different color characteristics. Cornish X birds were created for the sole purpose of producing meat. I sometimes like to call them "FrankenChickens." However, they do serve a great purpose, and they are incredibly quick growers for any homestead.

These hybrid chickens aren't typically very sustainable, meaning they don't often (or at all) efficiently reproduce their own offspring. And if they do, it won't be anything like their characteristics and body type.

Landrace chickens aren't really a breed at all. I know that's confusing, but it's important to understand exactly what they are before trying to seek them out. Landrace chickens are chickens that have grown and adapted by natural selection over centuries. These breeds weren't bred by a breeder—they were simply left to their own devices to survive. An example of landrace chickens are breeds such as the Icelandic, Swedish Flower Hen, and Olandsk Dwarf.

There isn't quite a standard conformation for landrace chickens like there is for heritage and hybrid breeds. They come in a kaleidoscope of colors and with various physical traits and patterns. While many will look similar in terms of feather coloring and pattern, this often depends on their country of origin.

These chickens have adapted well because of their strong survival instincts. They are often proficient layers and escape artists, especially if they aren't raised in slight confinement and handled often. They've survived this long on instinct, after all. Landraces are the closest you'll come to a wild bird in the chicken world. They are natural foragers, mothers, and protectors. When breeding landrace chickens, it's best to collect eggs and hatch from within your stock that is instinctively broody, alert, and quick on their feet! This means you hold back the best eggs from your best chickens so that you're continuing to breed and hatch the best characteristics.

My Favorite Homestead Breeds

One of the best parts of becoming a new chicken keeper is picking out the breeds that you want to raise. Now that you know whether you want a dual-purpose or an egg layer, or a heritage breed or a hybrid, the sky's the limit. Sometimes we just want "all the chickens."

Choosing the main breed on your property will depend on your needs and wants. If you just want a colorful egg basket, you can, by all means, throw a bunch of breeds together in your chicken run. But if you want to hatch your own eggs, you'll need to consider egg color mixes and pure breeding lines. We'll talk about that more in the

breeding section of the book.

In the meantime, let's walk through some of my very favorite breeds to have on the homestead.

Ameraucana. This light blue egg layer shouldn't be confused with the Americana or Easter Egger. True Ameraucanas lay only blue eggs and are derived from the Araucana chicken. Some people have great luck with this breed going broody, while others do not. They can be flighty if not handled often. They tend to lay every two days, though some lay once a day.

Australorp. This breed is the Australian version of an Orpington, but is common across the globe. They have beautiful black plumage and make the perfect peaceful pet. They are excellent brown egg layers and a dual-purpose breed.

Barnevelder. A brown egg layer, these chickens don't lay nearly as often as a sexlink, but will produce about three eggs per week. They are great dual-purpose birds and can be incredibly docile.

Brahma. Known originally as a vintage meat bird, this breed is a fabulous dual-purpose breed that lays brown eggs. It has long feathered leg shafts and puffy feathers. They are also fabulous brooders.

Cochin (large fowl and bantams). This docile breed lays only a couple of eggs each week, but they are extremely broody and entertaining. They're the perfect addition if you're looking for good mothers.

Delaware. Large brown eggs are this dual-purpose breed's specialty. Even in the twenty-first century, this bird is still used as a meat bird on many heritage homesteads. They are quiet and friendly, and even go broody every now and then. They are independent and great foragers.

Dominique. My grandmother raised Dominiques when she was a child, so they've always been special to me. Looking a lot like a Barred Plymouth Rock, this dual-purpose breed is the oldest breed in the United States. They are layers of large brown eggs and lay almost daily. They are calm and nurturing and can be great broody mamas.

Icelandic. A rare landrace, the addition of this breed to your property will bring with it a sense of accomplishment. Conserving this breed is special and necessary. They are naturally broody and lay daily, and even lay through most winters. They are more petite than regular large fowl, but are exceptionally good and broody mothers. They are also fantastic foragers, which means they aren't the biggest fans of confinement.

Java. Java and Dominique chickens are the two oldest breeds in the United States. In fact, many of the current USA breeds were derived from Javas. A hen from this rare, dual-purpose breed lays brown eggs a few times a week, is exceptionally docile, and is a fabulous broody mama.

Leghorn. While Leghorns are exceptional egg layers, they can be a little flighty. They are grand escape artists from predators, however. These white egg layers lay an egg daily and are great winter egg layers as well. Slightly on the petite side, they are very intelligent and active. This vintage commercial egg layer is a great addition to any flock if you're looking for a great heritage egg layer.

Marans (Black Copper, Blue, or Wheaten). Best known for their deep chocolate–colored eggs, this dual-purpose breed has a special place on my homestead. They are not very docile, but if handled frequently, they will become more submissive. They lay several eggs each week, and they can be great broody mothers.

Old English Game Fowl. While these birds are beautiful, they are especially wild. They are extremely self-sufficient and broody and are exceptional foragers. They don't do well in confinement, and lay just a couple of cream- or tinted-colored eggs each week. However, if you're looking for a self-sustaining homestead bird, this is it.

Orpington. One of my favorite breeds of all time, these sweethearts steal the heart of every chicken keeper known to mankind. They come in various colors and lay large brown eggs almost daily. They are excellent broody mamas and a fabulous dual-purpose breed. Orpingtons are extremely docile, and I often refer to them as "chicken puppies" because they follow you around everywhere!

Plymouth Rock. Another favorite on my homestead, this breed is spunky and entertaining. Much like Orpingtons, they are extremely docile when handled regularly, and they are very chatty. They lay large brown eggs almost daily and come in various colors. Depending on the lineage, they can be exceptional brooders.

Rhode Island Red. A dual-purpose brown egg layer that lays daily, this bird is a beautiful deep red color. They are fairly easygoing, but not good broodies. They are hearty and work well within confinement restrictions.

Sexlinks. There are plenty of sexlink breeds, and their main purpose is to lay eggs. Any sexlink works well on the homestead if you simply want a good, daily egg layer.

There are literally hundreds of breeds that you could choose from, but these breeds tend to be the most popular among chicken keepers and farmsteads, and for good reason, as you can see! As a chicken keeper, you may eventually decide to venture into more exotic and rare breeds, and that's where the real fun happens. But that's a story for another day.

Hatching, Purchasing, and Raising Chicks

LET'S START FROM THE VERY BEGINNING of a chicken's life—the egg and chick. Many chicken keepers choose to purchase hatching eggs or chicks, and most eventually get into hatching their own breeding stock. There are things to consider when purchasing eggs and chicks, and even before hatching your own.

Once those little peepers are into the brooder (you'll learn how to set that up in this section), what do you feed them? How do you ensure they don't get parasites? What happens if they *do* get sick? When can you move them to the big coop? These are all questions chicken keepers have.

There are a lot of natural ways to keep your chickens healthy from egg to juvenile, and we're going to go over most of them in this section. Not only will you learn how to keep them healthy, you'll learn how to hatch chicks, select healthy chicks from the farm store or breeder, care for growing chickens, prevent and treat common chick and juvenile bird issues, and even how to successfully tend to a broody hen and her chicks when nature decides to do the work for you!

CHAPTER

3

HATCHING AND PURCHASING CHICKS

I think it was a holiday—maybe Valentine's Day—when my husband brought home a giant box with "Styrofoam incubator" written on the side of it. The key to a farm girl's heart is farm animals, especially baby ones. This incubator not only meant I could hatch lots of poultry chicks whenever I wanted to, but it was also an incredible new tool to add to our homestead.

We like to use holidays as a way to get the things we actually need versus frivolous things that we don't (though I'll admit, I do love getting flowers!). We had already bought a few hens and chicks, and had even purchased French Black Copper Marans breeding stock, but now we needed to take the next step in our journey to self-sufficiency and chicken breeding—hatching our own eggs from our own lines.

My son was exceptionally excited to start this new adventure. Kids always love the hatching and chick stage in chicken keeping—little chicken keepers taking care of little chickens. It is one of the cutest things you'll ever experience and equally as exciting for adults as well.

Our first hatch was pretty successful, but we had a few mishaps here and there. Humidity was a big issue for me back in those

days, because I had no idea how important it was. Helping the chicks out of their shells was probably the next biggest issue for me! We have this drive to "help," when many times nature can work itself out.

Hatching eggs is a pretty simple process, but it can be extremely intimidating, and there are some important things you need to know. Let's walk through the process from start to finish, pinpointing some crucial elements you should consider. And if all else fails, after the hatching part, we'll talk about purchasing chicks if you think hatching isn't for you!

Choosing the Best Incubator

If you're ready to hatch your own chicks, you'll need to start by selecting the best incubator for you and your homestead. A lot of people think they should just go to their nearest farm store and buy the first incubator they find, but that isn't always the case.

Some chicken keepers have great success with one type of incubator, while others fail royally. Your incubator choice will depend on your lifestyle. If you're home all day and can babysit an incubator, a still air Styrofoam incubator would be a great choice for you—and it's pretty cheap! But if you're extremely busy and just want something you can set and forget, a forced air incubator with digital technology is a much better option for you.

While I'm at home all day on our property, I still opt for the digital version, because it's just one less thing to have to worry about!

There are three major types of incubator categories: still air incubator, forced/circulated air incubator, and heat/kerosene-powered incubator (or homemade). Each of these incubator categories have different subcategories, such as household incubators, box incubators, Styrofoam incubators, plastic incubators, cabinet incubators, mini-incubators, and more.

However, let's break down exactly how each main category of incubator works, as this will help you decide which category to start searching for your new 'bator.

Still Air Incubators

These incubators are the most common ones available at farm stores. They come with a heating element in the top portion of the incubator, windows, and air holes to help with ventilation. However, there isn't a fan to help circulate air, which means you can get cold spots in the incubator and have uneven hatch rates and times.

These incubators are often manual, which means you'll need to turn the eggs each day (two or three times a day) by yourself. You'll also need to buy a hygrometer to keep track of your humidity levels in the incubator. You'll learn about the proper humidity levels later in this section.

Suggested incubators: *Little Giant, Hova-Bator, Farm Innovators*

Forced/Circulated Air Incubators

These incubators are much easier to manage and keep track of. They have a fan that helps circulate the air so that there aren't any "cold" spots in the incubator—especially in the corners (if your 'bator has corners).

Forced air incubators often have digital mechanisms, where they turn the eggs for you (or have add-ons for egg turning), and keep track of the temperature and humidity, though not all have these features. Make sure you research each incubator.

These incubators are much more reliable with hatch rates and times. They are often "set and forget" incubators, which is nice for the busy homesteader!

Suggested incubators: *Hova-Bator, Brinsea*

Heat/Kerosene Incubators

If you're living off-grid without electricity (or if you're just looking for a fun project), these incubators might be a better option for you. However, they aren't as reliable as the other two incubator options already mentioned.

These incubators deal exclusively with manual heat. A kerosene incubator, for example, runs off of a kerosene lamp. This isn't necessarily the safest option unless you are home 90 percent of the day.

Not all heat incubators use fire, however. I've known plenty of people who create their own Styrofoam incubators at home, and their heat source is lightbulbs or a natural source—like sticking the incubator in the attic during warm seasons when hatching, or setting the incubator next to the woodstove in winter. This is a bit more work, but most certainly doable.

Of course, manually turning your eggs and maintaining steady heat and moisture levels makes this option more tedious than the commercial incubators.

Suggested incubators: Lehman's Kerosene Incubator, homemade Styrofoam incubator

Buying Quality Eggs or Selecting Your Own

You've chosen your breed. You've chosen your incubator. Next comes the eggs! You can't have chicks without eggs, right? This is, in my humble opinion, the part of hatching eggs that's the most fun. I can spend hours looking at breeders online and all of the beautiful eggs that they sell.

That's the question, though: Should you buy fertilized eggs from a breeder, or hatch your own?

Certainly, if you're just getting started, your eggs will have to come from somewhere. More likely than not, you'll need to find a reliable breeder or hatchery that sells hatching eggs. Reliable breeders can be found online through groups and forums, but you may try searching through breed associations first. Know the standard of the breed that you want, and then find your breeder or hatchery based on that standard.

If you're not picky about chicken breeds, any chicken keeper that has a rooster in their flock can offer you barnyard mix eggs for a reasonable price. If you're already buying eggs from a local chicken keeper to eat, and they have a rooster, chances are you can just hatch those eggs that

TIP

Incubators come in all different shapes and sizes—from incubators that hold six eggs to hundreds of eggs (cabinet incubators), there's something for everyone. As your needs grow, your incubators will grow!

TIP

If you're not picky about quality, by all means go with the commercial hatcheries. However, if you're looking to hatch chicks that are to breed standard, find a reliable breeder or purchase from a hatchery that imports new birds every few years.

you've bought that week if they haven't been washed or refrigerated. I don't often suggest this, however, unless you know the chicken keeper well.

Always know where your chickens are coming from—and that includes your hatching eggs. Different diseases and bacteria can be transferred to embryos from the flock, so it's extremely important to know where your future flock is coming from.

How to Tell If an Egg Is Fertilized

If you have eggs of your own, there's an easy trick to tell if your chicken's eggs are fertilized or not. In the photo, you can see a white bull's-eye on the egg yolk. The dot makes a perfect circle with a small dot inside of it. This perfect circle is the first sign of life in this precious little egg. When you see the bull's-eye perfect circle, you can assume your rooster is doing its job and your eggs are fertile! If the egg just has a white, nonsymmetrical spot, it's not fertile. I wouldn't suggest cracking open eggs that you've bought from a breeder to check fertility, however. Just stick them in the incubator and watch them grow!

If you've bought your eggs from a breeder, they will typically select quality eggs to send you from their flock. But if you're using your own eggs, you'll need to go through an egg selection process with a few helpful hints to finding good and bad eggs.

How to Select and Prepare Hatching Eggs
Choose Less Porous Eggs
Most chicken eggs are naturally porous, but there's a difference between a normally

Egg on left is extremely porus, egg on right is normal.

porous egg and an extremely porous egg. The calcium in eggshells naturally deposits itself thicker and thinner on certain areas of the egg. But if your chickens aren't getting enough calcium and protein in their diet, their eggs can become extremely thin and brittle. This doesn't make for a good hatching egg, as bacteria can sneak into the eggshell.

You'll need to select the least porous eggs that you can find. You can do this by candling the egg (holding a flashlight up to the egg) and selecting the eggs that have less light coming through the thin spots. Typically, darker eggs are less porous than light-colored eggs, but sometimes you're only hatching light-colored eggs, so choose the less porous ones.

Choose Eggs That Are a Good Size and Color

Your best eggs are the eggs that are generally very symmetrical, round, not very pointy, and have the best overall appearance in size and color according to breed. If you're breeding your own chickens and trying to enhance color, choose the best-colored eggs. All of these things will allow the chicken to have enough room to grow and maintains excellent egg conformation and color in future generations.

Choose Eggs without Cracks or Dents

This is a given, but often cracks can be overlooked since they are so small. Inspect each egg while candling them for porousness, making sure there aren't any hairline fractures in the eggshell.

Choose the Cleanest Eggs

Let's get real here: Chickens poop everywhere, including their nesting boxes. Sometimes there can be a little chicken poop on eggs. Oftentimes there's also mud, especially during the rainy seasons. Try to choose the cleanest eggs you can find, because you definitely don't want to wash the eggs. Here's why . . .

Never Wash Your Hatching Eggs

There is a natural protective bloom on the outside of your chicken eggs, which helps keep bacteria out of the egg. Because we know that eggs are naturally porous, any time an egg is washed, it can allow that liquid to seep into the eggshell. This is often how hatching eggs get bad bacteria inside of them, causing hatches to be a failure.

Natural Incubator Cleaner

Before you put your precious eggs into that incubator, it's best to give it a good washing and then allow it to air-dry completely. Don't use those harsh chemicals, though! All you need are a few simple ingredients:

White vinegar

Water

Tea tree essential oil

In a small bowl, mix equal parts vinegar and water, then add 5 to 10 drops of quality tea tree (or melaleuca) essential oil, which is a natural antibacterial. With a clean rag, wash your incubator down with this mixture, being sure not to get any mechanical parts wet. Use this mixture to clean out your incubator after a hatch as well! If you don't have tea tree essential oil, just use straight white vinegar without the water.

All right, here we go. We've chosen our eggs, now we are ready to incubate! Depending on the incubator you've chosen, this process should be pretty painless. But as always, there are some tips and tricks to ensuring a successful hatch!

Incubating Your Eggs

Setting Eggs in the Incubator

If you've bought hatching eggs from a breeder, or have had them shipped to you, you'll need to *allow the eggs to rest for about 12 hours*, pointy end down or naturally sitting on the counter. I do this with my own eggs as well. This ensures that the air sac rises to the proper end of the egg.

While your eggs are resting, *preheat your incubator* at least 12 to 24 hours in advance. You'll also need to pour water into the humidity wells of the incubator. Don't fill them up all the way right away, however. You may only need a little water for humidity, depending on the season and your location.

Don't be like me (the first and fifth time) and just throw the eggs in the incubator while it's heating up. This is especially important for still air incubators, as you could ruin your hatching eggs if the heat gets too hot.

Before placing your eggs into the incubator, mark an X on one side of the egg and an O on the other. Use a pencil to do this, so as not to allow ink to get into the egg,

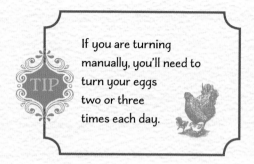

further increasing your risk of contamination. Why do you do this? Well, if you're turning your eggs manually, this will help you see which eggs have been turned and which ones haven't. I do this for my automatically turned eggs as well so that I can make sure my egg turner is working.

I turn my eggs first thing in the morning and once in the evening. If you're home during the day, you can turn them around lunchtime as well. This ensures that the embryo doesn't become attached to one side of the egg.

Now that your eggs are ready, carefully place them in the incubator, close the top, and wait 1 hour for your temperature and humidity to come back up. After an hour, if your humidity levels and temperature need to be adjusted, do so accordingly. However, don't freak out if they are just a few points or degrees off. Your temperature and humidity levels will constantly change. Just make sure they haven't drastically changed during incubation (no more than 2 to 3 degrees above or below).

The Incubation Process

Over the next 17 days, it's going to be pretty uneventful. However, there are some things to look forward to, like candling your eggs. It's kind of like an ultrasound for chickens! You don't want to candle them often, however, as it is an opportunity for bacteria to transfer from your hands to your eggs.

Here's a general candling schedule that I go by:

Day 7: Check to see that each egg has embryonic growth. If you aren't seeing any growth at all in the egg at this point (it's extremely clear with no veining), it's safe to say that you can toss it. If in doubt, you can hold it a few more days, but just be careful. You don't want to keep these eggs in the incubator if they aren't viable, as they can explode and contaminate the other eggs.

Day 14: Candle the eggs to ensure that all embryos are still growing. Sometimes you'll notice that an embryo hasn't grown since day 7. If that's the case, again, toss it out. The embryo has died for an unknown reason, or because of bacteria transfer.

If I'm super-excited about a hatch, sometimes I'll check again around day 17, before lockdown (see "How Many Days?" sidebar below), but I typically try not to. At this point, it's practically impossible to see anything, as the chick fills most of the egg.

How Many Days?

It generally takes 21 days for chicken eggs to hatch. Note that smaller eggs, like bantams, can hatch on day 18. When we raised Icelandic chickens, they typically hatched on days 18 and 19. Keep this in mind when calculating your lockdown day. Once day 18 arrives, you'll need to keep the lid of your incubator shut at all times, up your humidity, and try your best not to open that lid again! This is what we refer to as "lockdown day." The extra humidity is needed so that the membrane in the shell doesn't get stuck to the chick, and allows the chick to move about more freely so that it can hatch.

The Hatching Process

It's finally day 21, and we're ready to hatch these babies! At first you'll see a little pip in the shell. This is a slight puncture to the eggshell where the chick pecks into the air sac to start the hatching process.

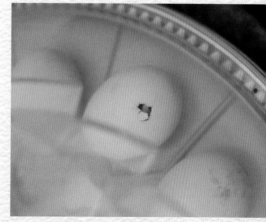

Chicks can take 24-plus hours to completely hatch. While it's extremely tempting to try to help them, allow them at least 24 hours to hatch on their own before you begin to intervene. Some chicks simply pip early. Most eggs will begin hatching all at once, but I've had the incubator going for 2 to 3 days before all of our chicks have hatched.

When your chick is ready to emerge into the world, it will zip a line around the egg and then pop the top off when it's ready to come out. Just like that, you're a chicken keeper to a brand-new generation of chickens!

Helping Chicks Hatch

While it is often said that you should never help chicks hatch, we do make an exception here on our homestead. Sometimes some chicks are just too big to hatch from their shells. Other times the humidity drops and the chicks become "shrink-wrapped" by the inner membrane and can't get out. You should always give the chick 24 to 28 hours to hatch on its own, but after that, it might be time to intervene.

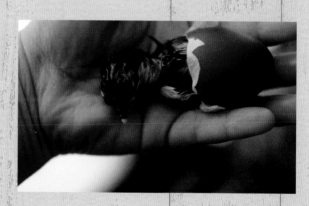

You can do this by mimicking the "zip" around the egg. Very carefully take tweezers and start chipping away at the eggshell, being sure not to hit the chick itself. Once the egg is fully zipped, place the egg back into the incubator and allow the chick to do the remainder of the work. The chick should, eventually, pop right out. It could take a few hours or a few minutes.

Never force the chick to come out unless you're certain the chick is simply too weak to do so on its own. When helping chicks hatch, you run the risk of causing the chick to hatch too soon. This can cause the chick to bleed excessively from the veins in the shell, or cause the egg yolk not to be completely absorbed, allowing bacteria into the chick's body. This is why we always suggest waiting until the final moments to help hatch.

Allow the chicks to stay in the incubator until they are completely dry and fluffed up. This is an extremely important rule to heed, as not only does it ensure your humidity levels stay intact for the other chicks that are hatching, but it also encourages other chicks to hatch when they hear their chick-friends peeping! Once your chicks are completely dry, place them in the brooder that you've set up (we'll talk about that shortly).

If you aren't ready to take on hatching as a new chicken keeping skill, then purchasing chicks is your next option, and my goodness, what a great option it is!

Purchasing Chicks from the Farm Store, Hatchery, or Breeder

It's officially that time of year—early spring. You see the signs all over the place, "Chick Days Are Here," but you cringe because you know you don't have room for any more chicks. Or, maybe you don't have any chicks at all, and this is the day you want to add them to your backyard or farmstead.

Here we go. Deep breaths. *Try not to buy all the chicks*, you tell yourself. And somehow, some way, you're absolutely going to fail . . . and you'll buy more chicks than you should've. It's called chicken addiction, OK? It's a disease, I tell you!

All kidding aside, purchased chicks are, in many ways, a lot easier for the chicken keeper to start or maintain a flock. Hatching eggs can present challenges, and the wait isn't ideal for people who lack patience. So, we often opt to purchase chicks, either at our local farm store, from a hatchery, or through a breeder.

Choosing your breed may be your first step, but choosing where to purchase your chicks is equally as important.

The Farm Store

Your local farm store will most likely carry chicks every single spring and fall. Most homesteaders replenish their flocks during these times of the year. These chicks normally come from hatcheries, though some farm stores carry locally hatched and raised chicks.

Pros: Many times the farm store will have straight-run chicks or pullet chicks. This is especially convenient if you are just looking for pullets. They generally carry the most common breeds, including heritage breeds, sexlinks, and bantams.

Cons: The trip from the hatchery to the farm store and then to your home can be a bit stressful on chicks. This is where "pasty butt" in chicks begins to cause issues. (We'll talk about pasty butt in Chapter 4.) Oftentimes the stress from constant transportation can cause a higher death rate than if you were ordering from the hatchery straight to your home, or directly from a breeder. The farm store doesn't always have all of the breeds you may want, either, as they generally only carry main breeds that are the most popular that year. Another con: You don't have the option to look over the chicks. The farm store will normally just put chicks in a box without allowing you to touch them, according to state law, and for good reason. Most people don't know how to handle chicks properly. While farm stores won't allow you to pick up chicks and look them over when you purchase them, you can certainly request for them to choose chicks that are naturally alert, plump, and without pasty butt. Final con: You normally have to purchase four to six chicks minimum, depending on the store. So if you're just wanting two chicks, you might be out of luck. However, the laws have recently changed, and now there is no minimum number of chicks you must buy unless they are for pets only. Check with your local extension office first, and keep in mind that stores can designate what the minimum amount to purchase is even if there legally is no minimum.

The Hatchery

Hatcheries are a great option if you're looking to purchase chicks in bulk, you are interested in a certain breed, or you want the convenience of shopping online. You can order straight-run or pullet, and different hatcheries offer different breeds. Most generic hatcheries offer the same types of breeds, but there are also some high-quality hatcheries that breed imported birds that are more highly sought after.

Pros: You can shop at home in your pajamas, and you don't have to worry about transporting the chicks from a different location except from the post office. You'll find more breeds, including rarer breeds.

Cons: Typically the box will come to you unharmed, but other times the box might turn up damaged with injured chicks. This isn't common, but it can happen. Due to transportation, you also run the risk of opening up the box to find dead chicks. While this isn't typically a traumatic event for an adult, it may be something to consider with children around. This is a step that the farm store does eliminate when they receive hatchery chicks. Another con: You won't have a chance to look over the chicks. You're simply at the mercy of whatever they send you. And the last con: Some hatcheries require you purchase ten or more chicks per order.

The Trusted Breeder

My favorite way to purchase chicks is from a trusted and reliable breeder. I say this both as a chicken keeper and as a chicken breeder. It may take a bit longer, and may cost a bit more, but if you're searching for a certain breed or egg color, finding a reliable breeder is best. They can ship the eggs to you just as a hatchery would, and they are just a phone call away if you have any questions. You can also find extremely rare chicken breeds that are top quality.

Pros: Breeder chicks are typically of higher quality than hatchery chicks, both in conformation and egg shape and color quality. Many breeders keep track of their breeding lines, and this is a great way to learn where your chicken flock came from. A great pro is that you typically get to look over the chicks you're purchasing from a local breeder. This isn't the case, though, if you're purchasing from a distant breeder.

Cons: It's extremely hard, and time-consuming, to find a trusted and reliable breeder. As with any backyard animal breeder, sometimes chickens can be overbred with bad quality, or bred too closely in relation to one another. Start by finding a breeder through the American Poultry Association, or through the specific breed associations that you are part of.

No matter where you decide to get your chicks, you'll always want to check them over as thoroughly as possible when you receive them.

Natural "Electrolyte" Pick-Me-Up

Sometimes chicks need a pick-me-up drink after all that transporting. Instead of buying electrolytes at the store, which can sometimes have too much salt in them, mix the following into their quart waterer:

1 tablespoon raw honey

1 teaspoon apple cider vinegar

1 smashed garlic clove

1 handful fresh thyme

Once you receive your chicks, you'll want to make sure you have a brooder set up. Get them into the pre-warmed brooder as quickly as possible with fresh feed, water, warm bedding, and even some herbs!

Brooders

Setting Up the Brooder

A brooder is something that's semipermanent—maybe just a cardboard box—until you move your chicks into something more permanent, like a coop. Different chicken keepers enjoy different brooder options. You'll find what works best for you and your space limitations.

For the first week, we typically keep our chicks indoors in a cardboard box or storage container. For the first three to seven days, we don't use any bedding at all. Instead, we use paper towels. It's easier to clean out the brooders this way rather than constantly cleaning out bedding.

You can use a secured heat lamp indoors, but I do suggest looking into a warming pad or EcoGlow convection heater instead. These electrical heat sources keep the chicks warm without the danger of using a heat lamp. The only con is that they don't work well in outdoor brooders if the temperature is too cold. Use these heaters in temperatures above 60°F.

Herbs for the Brooder

From the very beginning of their lives, I offer herbs and natural options to my chicks. Here are some of the fresh and dry herbs that we offer, free choice, and why we use them:

Thyme: helps eradicate parasites, is antifungal and antibacterial (fresh in feed or infused in water)

Oregano: antibacterial, stimulates the immune system (fresh in feed or infused in water)

Astragalus: stimulates the immune system, antibacterial, may prevent avian influenza (dried, infused in water)

Garlic: promotes digestion, antibacterial, antiparasitic (minced dried in feed or fresh in water)

Not only are these herbs great for the chicks' digestive system, but they give them something to peck and rub and create a pleasant chicken experience.

After their first week in the indoor brooder, we tend to move our chicks to our outdoor brooder. We'll talk about this in a second. However, if you keep your chicks

in an indoor brooder until they are mostly feathered, you'll need to gradually raise the heat lamp or brooder heater farther and farther away from the chicks after the first week, until they no longer need it. This allows them to get acclimated to the ambient temperatures so that the change in heat isn't a stress on their bodies.

Once chicks are completely feathered between 6 and 8 weeks of age, they can go outside without any heat at all. However, I suggest not adding them to your larger flock until they are between 8 and 12 weeks of age, depending on

the breed, due to the pecking order in your flock and the simple fact that chicks can get trampled.

The Outdoor Brooder

We really enjoy having an outdoor brooder because, let's face it, chicks aren't the best-smelling thing in the world. After the first week of being indoors and getting used to us, we move our chicks to an outdoor brooder near our chicken coop. The outdoor brooder is basically a mini–chicken coop that we've converted into a brooder. We stuff it full of straw and then place a regular floodlight bulb (65 watt) in the lamp base. Because the lamp is so close to the floor, the chicks can snuggle up to the lamp and keep warm as little or as often as they like. We don't use a heat lamp in our brooder for the simple reason that it is extremely dangerous and can catch the brooder on fire with the straw in a confined area.

The outdoor brooder has a small covered run off the housing area, and this allows our chicks to transition with the regular flock on a daily basis rather than having to transition them once they are bigger. They can mingle with the flock from the protected chick run until they are big enough to be integrated into the regular flock.

What You Should Have in Your Brooder

Whether you opt for an indoor or outdoor brooder, each brooder needs a few special things to make it a healthy and nurturing environment for your chicks, such as:

- **Feed, water, and supplements.** You'll be feeding your chicks twice a day and giving them clean water at least that many times as well. There are also some supplements you should consider, and we'll list those in the next chapter.

- **Clean bedding.** Choose clean bedding for your chicks to have in their brooder. We opt for wood shavings or straw, depending on the season and location of the brooder.

- **A dust bathing area.** Chicks will begin trying to take a dust bath as early as 1 week old. Create a dust bathing area in the brooder with dirt, sand, and diatomaceous earth (or wood ash) so that your chicks can keep themselves clean and bug-free!

- **A roost.** Eventually your chicks will start learning how to roost. Provide platforms or small roosting bars for them to sleep on.

Make sure your brooder is sturdy and easy to clean. After a certain age, chicks will most certainly make a major mess. You'll constantly be cleaning and replacing bedding, and giving them fresh water multiple times a day!

Now that you have the basics down, let's start talking about raising chicks naturally, especially when it comes to their diet and surroundings. In the next chapter you'll discover just how enjoyable this chicken-raising process is about to become, and how you can incorporate herbs and natural chicken keeping into your flock.

CHAPTER 4

RAISING CHICKS NATURALLY

The first set of chicks we raised on our homestead came from one of our neighbors. She hatched eight precious little Barred Rock chicks for us, and we had absolutely no idea what we were doing. I sat for hours—with my then-toddler son in my lap—watching these little chicks run around, pecking at their own feet, jumping into our hands, and making little peeping sounds.

Wouldn't you know, five out of eight of those chicks were roosters? But they were the best roosters. They followed my little one

around the yard all day every day. They would work on his bike with him, thinking that maybe he'd pull out a worm in the process. They were the most curious things, and they thought he was just one of the fellas.

We lost two of the chicks for unknown reasons. Back then, I had no clue this was a natural process when it came to chicks. Certainly, there are those who've never lost a chick in their entire lives (though I'd dare challenge that), but I am here to assure you that it is extremely common to lose at least one chick out of every batch. It's just the natural occurrence of the circle of life with these fragile creatures.

Chicks will eventually grow up and become an incredible resource on your homestead—protective roosters and egg-laying hens. Whether it's for entertainment purposes—like the roosters helping a toddler clean a bike—or as a sustainable egg or meat resource on your property, these chicks need to start their holistic care from day one.

We've gone over herbs in the brooder box in the previous chapter, but what about their feed and water? What if they get parasites or dreaded coccidiosis as a chick? These are very real concerns for the new chicken keeper, so let's talk about it!

Natural Chick Feed, Water, and Supplements

Chicks are pretty simple when it comes to their feed. Offering them a good-quality, non-medicated organic crumble feed will do the trick. You can purchase this feed, or if you're in a more rural area, sometimes you'll be able to get non–genetically modified organism (GMO) feed milled right at your local farm store. This means that the plants in the food haven't been genetically engineered. Make sure the protein percentage is right around 19 percent. This will help the chicks through the feather-growing process, as growing feathers takes a lot of protein!

Offering your chicks fresh water multiple times each day will ensure that they get enough clean water to flush out their digestive tracts. One of the biggest issues with parasites and bacteria in the chick's digestive tract is due to unclean water, soiled areas in the brooder, or contaminated dirt.

Besides the regular feed and water, here are some other things you should consider offering your chicks for a natural and healthy diet:

Grit. These tiny particles of small rocks, sand, and other natural gritty material can be bought or found in nature. Because chickens don't have teeth, their gizzard grinds up all of their food for them, with the help of grit and small stones that they may pick up along the way. If your chicks aren't touching soil each day, this means they aren't going to be getting enough grit. Take your chicks out for supervised and contained ranging to get grit straight from the soil you walk on. Otherwise, purchase a small bag of grit for them at your local farm store.

Thyme, oregano, and garlic.
Since you're opting for a natural diet for your chicks, make sure you're giving them these herbs a couple of times each week in their feed or water to help prevent parasites and bacterial issues naturally. I like to hang bundles from the top of the brooder so that they can peck at the herbs. Otherwise, I enjoy making infusions a couple of times each week to give to them in their waterer.

> ### MAKE AN HERBAL INFUSION!
> Make an herbal water infusion by steeping 1 teaspoon each of dried thyme, oregano, and garlic in 2 cups of almost boiling water, as if you were making a tea. Then strain out the herbs, and once the water has cooled a bit, offer the infusion to your chicks in their 12-ounce waterer. Change out this infusion every 10 to 12 hours, offering it to your chicks two or three times each week.
>
>
>
> *TIP*

Mealworms. These dried creatures are a great treat and boredom buster for chicks. It's exceptionally entertaining to watch the chicks run around with little mealworms in their mouths, playing "keep-away" with their chick roomies. The mealworms are also a great source of protein, which helps the chicks during the growth of their feathers. You can toss in a handful a couple of times each week as a treat.

Astragalus. This immune-stimulating herb is always in my herbal livestock remedies cabinet, and it is especially something that I love giving my chicks to help their fragile immune systems. Create a decoction out of the astragalus root and offer it to your chicks once a week to support a healthy immune system and for its antibacterial properties. You can create a decoction by boiling 1 tablespoon of shredded astragalus root in 2 cups of water for 10 minutes, then strain out the astragalus root and place the water in the chick's waterer. Replace after 12 hours.

Raw apple cider vinegar (ACV). The good bacteria in raw organic ACV are extremely beneficial to the chicken's digestive tract and overall health. Add 1 tablespoon of raw organic ACV to 1 gallon of water a couple of times each week for general health maintenance.

Fresh grass clippings and bugs. In an effort to maintain a natural environment, we really enjoy adding tufts of grass, dirt, and bugs that we find to the chick brooder. This acclimates the chicks to a natural environment if they aren't on pasture in their brooder.

There are certainly other commercial treats and items you could give them, but at the chick stage, I prefer to keep it plain and simple on their brand-new digestive systems so that I can monitor them more easily. As they grow into mature birds, you'll see that there are other things we begin to add into the mix.

Common Chick Ailments, Natural Preventatives, and Treatments

As with any animal or human, we sometimes worry most about how to naturally treat an illness. What if they get sick? Is it possible to treat an illness or bacterial infection with natural remedies? While the answer isn't as black-and-white as you may think, there are quite a few ways to help prevent illness and disease in your little flock, starting with the suggested diet that we just went over. Should they contract an illness or ailment, I have some natural remedies for you as well.

Prevention is key when it comes to using natural remedies. A preventative and integrative routine will help keep your growing flock in tip-top shape. Some things, however, can't be prevented very well, but luckily we have natural treatments for that.

Let's break it down by common chick ailments, how to prevent them, and how to treat them should they come about. While the list of things that could be ailing your chicks is extensive, I've only included some of the most common ailments. Most other ailments are extremely rare in the natural chicken keeper's world, but besides that, there are plenty of educational resources out there strictly dedicated to chicken ailments (you'll find some in the resources section at the back of this book).

Brooder Pneumonia (Aspergillosis)

This ailment is a respiratory issue in chickens and other fowl. It is typically started by *Aspergillus fumigatus*, a common fungus. Chicks can come in contact with this fungus in incubators harboring the fungus or when inhaling spores from wet or moldy bedding. Symptoms include respiratory distress, gasping for air, tremors, lack of appetite, and weight loss.

Prevention: Make sure your chicks are brooding in an area where their bedding isn't constantly wet or soiled. Offer them a decoction or infusion of astragalus and echinacea to boost their immune system once a week.

Treatment: Lemongrass, eucalyptus, cinnamon, cassia, garlic, and holy basil essential oils have all been scientifically proven to combat fungal and viral issues. In addition, in a 2012 study, *Loxostylis alata* A. Spreng, ex Rchb. extract (also known as wild pepper tree, tigerwood, or tarwood) was proven to have exceptional antifungal properties, specifically to rid poultry of brooder pneumonia. While this herb can be difficult to find, it may be worth having an extract on hand for when you need it. However, we can get similar benefits from the essential oils mentioned above. Place 1 drop of each essential oil in a glass bowl or bottle, and add 10 drops of fractionated coconut oil or carrier oil of your choice. Place a toothpick into the mixture and then apply the oil on the end of the toothpick directly on the skin of the chest or under the wing of your chick(s). Do this every day for 1 week, then every few days until symptoms subside. Make sure you're offering an immune-boosting herb, like astragalus, in their waterer to help their immune system.

Coccidiosis

One of the most common ailments in chicks, this bacteria is vicious once it infects them, and it spreads like wildfire. Chicks and chickens can contract cocci through everyday foraging or in wet foraging areas. Symptoms include bloody feces, loss of appetite, pale wattles and combs, acting chilled or huddling together, diarrhea, dehydration, and lethargy.

Tip

Chickens typically become immune to the coccidiosis bacteria once they have gotten it, so try to breed for resistance from those chickens in the future if you have a breeding program. It's also important to understand that chicks, at some point, need to come into contact with cocci in order to build up immunity. Add clumps of dirt to your brooder from day one to help naturally introduce the bacteria to them.

Prevention: Keeping your chick's bedding and foraging area clean and dry is important. Cocci typically spreads through excessively wet bedding or living conditions, where the bacteria can live and grow. I give my chicks the electrolyte mixture on page 48 as a cocci preventative almost daily, until their immune systems are strong enough to combat it on their own. Apple cider vinegar in their waterer helps as well.

Treatment: Wormwood, garlic, chicory, and black walnut hulls all have antiparasitic and antibacterial properties. Create a tincture out of these to keep on hand when you need it. Find the antibacterial and antiviral tincture recipe on page 160.

Pasty Butt

This is the most common chick ailment that almost every single chicken keeper will have to deal with at some time or another. Pasting occurs when chicks become stressed, either from not having the proper diet or heating conditions or from having too much sugar or additives in their waterer. Symptoms are very specific and noticeable, including feces stuck to the feathers and vent of the chick. It will start as a runny dropping, but then harden into a large glob. If left untreated, it can cause death.

Prevention: Create a stress-free brooder by making sure your chicks are always warm enough and getting enough nutrition. Offer apple cider vinegar and astragalus to their waterer to help them adapt to stress.

Treatment: The treatment for pasty butt is very simple. Wet the area where the feces is stuck and gently pull off all of the fecal matter once it begins to loosen from the vent. Put a bit of herbal antibacterial ointment (see page 154) on the vent to help soothe and prevent more sticking from occurring. Add the apple cider vinegar and astragalus to their waterer to help them adapt to stress if you'd like, though this is not required.

Rot Gut (Necrotic enteritis)

This issue, just like many other chicken ailments, is bacterial. While it is mostly common in broiler flocks, it can happen with layers as well. Symptoms include loss of appetite, listlessness, diarrhea, slow growth, and sudden death.

Prevention: Make sure your chicks are living in dry brooders. Bacteria spreads and grows rapidly in wet living conditions. Boost their immune system at the first sign of droopiness or loss of appetite by adding astragalus and echinacea, as well as thyme since it's a natural antiparasitic. I would highly recommend added a natural yeast or probiotic to your chick feed as well, as it helps even out good and bad intestinal bacteria.

Treatment: Create the antibacterial and antiviral tincture on page 160 and add to the waterer once a day until symptoms subside. Add dried or brewer's yeast to your chick feed to help even out good and bad bacteria in the intestinal tract, or offer a natural probiotic.

Spraddle Leg

While this isn't a sickness or disease, spraddle leg (or splay leg) is a common issue that many chicks deal with. Chicks get spraddle leg when they are brooded on a slick surface and can't catch their grip well when they are first starting to walk. Other causes could be a vitamin deficiency or from the chick being positioned awkwardly in the egg.

Prevention: Brood your chicks on a non-slippery surface like wood shavings, shredded newspaper, or paper towels.

Treatment: Tape the two legs together with a bandage or medical wrap, leaving a gap where the leg gap would typically be. A general rule of thumb is that you could use an adhesive bandage, and make the width between the legs the same width as the white sterile pad on the bandage, then wrap the sticky portion of the bandage around the legs. This will strengthen the chick's legs and cause the chick to walk normally. Add vitamins and minerals to your chick's waterer, as well as homemade electrolytes (page 48) to help keep your chick active and stable.

Wry Neck

There is no rhyme or reason as to how or why chickens get wry neck (or crooked neck), but there are ways to help treat the issue. Some believe that wry neck happens

when there is a vitamin deficiency. Others suspect bacterial issues or even just plain genetics. There's really no way to prevent it in chicks since we're not sure what the exact cause is, but we can help treat it.

Treatment: Add additional minerals and vitamins to your chick's waterer, along with the homemade electrolyte recipe in this book (page 48), until symptoms subside (this can take up to 1 week).

Raising Juvenile Chickens

After the first week, you'll notice a lot more feathers on your chicks. By the second week, there will be even more. By the fourth week of age, chicks should be completely off the heat lamp as long as the outdoor and indoor temperatures remain at or above 60°F.

We continue to give the dietary supplements that we give to our younger chicks, but right around 6 to 8 weeks of age, I like to incorporate a few kitchen scraps into their daily routine. Scraps like vegetables, eggs, and meat are a favorite among most chicks. They also do a lot more supervised free-ranging, either in an enclosed pasture pen or for an hour while I'm outside doing chores.

Here's what you can expect, week by week, as your chickens and juvenile birds grow out:

Weeks 2 to 3: You'll begin noticing a lot more wing and back feathers. At this age they are flying around and jumping whenever they get the chance. They are extremely active, taking in a lot more food and water than normal. Make sure you are cleaning out their brooder often, as they are going to be excreting feces a lot more often as well!

Weeks 4 to 5: They think they know it all at this age—not much different from human babies! They're extra-curious about you, but they think it's cool to run off on their own as well—though, in moments of insecurity, they are still going to be glued right to your side. Some of your chicks, especially bantams, might be almost completely feathered out by this age. If you haven't already, you should consider moving them to an outdoor brooder. The ammonia in their feces is now almost unbearable since they are relieving themselves quite often now.

Weeks 6 to 9: Your babies aren't such babies anymore. By week 8 they are completely feathered and look like miniature adult chickens. If given the chance, they would be right with the big boy and girl flock. An outdoor brooder is your best bet during this age. Consider an outdoor brooder that has a run off of it that is highly protected on all sides and on top. If you have a current flock of chickens, you might consider placing the brooder in with your other chickens or coop, in a safe place, so that your chicks can begin getting accustomed to your flock, and your flock to its new members. You won't want to transition your chicks until around 8 to 10 weeks of age, because they need a little time to accustom themselves to the other chickens before you let them loose in the hen house.

Now is the time to start introducing a raw food diet other than just pasture. Leftover raw veggies, oatmeal (in moderation), crushed eggshells, leftover scrambled eggs, Chaffhaye alfalfa, soaked or fermented feed (see instructions in Chapter 6) and other natural non-processed foods in smaller pieces work well.

Note: If you are raising meat chicks, now is the time when you'll consider processing those birds.

Weeks 10 to 20: Your babies have left the nest . . . flown the coop . . . gotten out of Dodge! They are ready to roam the pasture with their flock companions at the beck and call of the worms and bugs crawling up through the soil. They want to feel the grass beneath their feet! If you have bantams, these chicks may start laying around week 19 or 20.

It's important to know that at this age, your chicks should start transitioning over to a layer crumble or pellet. From weeks 12 through 14, transition your chicks over to your preferred layer feed by offering them half-and-half feed (old and new feed types) and gradually decreasing their old feed over the course of a week or so, until they are completely eating their new adult chicken feed. It's important to begin boosting that protein and getting a good organic or non-GMO layer feed into them before they begin laying eggs in a few weeks.

Weeks 21 to 24: If you are raising egg layers, this is the most exciting age for you. Most egg layers begin laying their eggs around the 21- to 24-week mark, depending on the size of the bird and the breed. Bantams and smaller-bodied breeds will lay a few weeks earlier than regular breeds.

Important: Your chickens should be on a quality layer feed at least a month before they begin laying eggs so that they get enough calcium and protein to create their golden nuggets of goodness for you! On our homestead, we also incorporate a raw feed diet. You can learn more about adult chickens' dietary needs and feeding methods in Chapter 6.

Transitioning Your Chicks into an Existing Flock

Some chicken keepers like to wait until 14 to 15 weeks of age to transition juvenile chickens into an established flock, but I've found that, if given the proper amount of transition time, chicks that don't grow up with a broody hen can easily be integrated starting at the 10-week mark.

You'll want to integrate chicks over the course of a few days. Place your juvenile birds into a large dog crate or separate area within your current chicken run. It's easier to make a little housing area with a run off of it so that your chicks can put themselves away at night, or you can move the dog crate into the big coop at night.

Allow the chickens to get accustomed to the new flock members over the course of 2 to 3 days. When the time is right, place the new chicks into the chicken coop on the roosts in the evening after your chickens have gone to roost. The next morning, they will integrate into the flock.

Don't worry, there will be a few pecks and picks here and there. This is a natural way for chickens to establish a pecking order. Within a few days, they will be just like the rest of the flock and will have transitioned well!

Important: If at any time you do see excessive picking, to the point of drawing blood or injury, try the transition period for a few more days, or isolate the bully in the established chicken flock until the new members are integrated. While this is rare, it can happen at times.

I should warn you—once you've raised your first batch of chicks, you'll want to do it over and over again, especially if you've hatched your own. My husband often says, "No. Walk past the bins full of chicks, babe." And when he sees me eyeing my incubator, he's often quick to remind me that I already have chickens that I don't need!

There is a good balance between having what you need and needing what you have. That's the beauty of chicks—we need chicks in our lives. It's just a given. Sometimes husbands don't get that!

When I'm feeling super-sneaky though, I let the chicken do the hatching for me. There is an art to the broody hen, and we'll learn all about that next.

A BROODY HEN AND HER CHICKS

There was a slight chill in the air that morning. I remember, because the sweatshirt I had on was the kind that keeps you just a little *too* warm for comfort, but if you took it off, you'd freeze. My husband Mark and I had been driving around looking for our next stop: chicken legend Harvey Ussery's home. He had told me that he lived right in town, near the post office, but knowing the amount of poultry he had, for some odd reason, I just didn't believe him.

We were on our way to purchase some Icelandic chicken hatching eggs from him. He is one of the greatest chicken mentors who has walked the earth, in my humble opinion. So to say I was excited is an understatement.

We finally found the place, and lo and behold, it was right smack-dab in the middle of town. It was a humble little cottage property with large open grassy areas of pasture, more than big enough for chickens. His property was surrounded by trees and some privacy brush. This was chicken heaven.

I knocked on the side door, and he welcomed us with open arms. It was like seeing an old friend again, except this was the first time we had met. Even though we were in a time crunch, he insisted on showing us his setups and chickens. His was a soul eager and willing to share all of his knowledge with you, even if you didn't ask for it. We gladly soaked it all up like a dry sponge!

We toured his large barn that was split into three sections for breeding (which we'll talk about later), but the thing that was most intriguing to me was the "broody barn," a small area completely dedicated to broody hens.

Harvey believes in the complete and total sustainability of chicken keeping, as do most homesteaders, and I was instantly inspired to mimic the success he had with raising broody hens and allowing them to hatch chicks. He explained to us that not all chickens are created equal, and that even in naturally broody breeds, broodies still need a little nurturing to set them on the proper path of being successful chicken mamas.

Everything I learned that day I brought home to try out myself on my own broodies. And my goodness, what a difference it has made.

Over the years, broodiness has been bred out of many breeds that are sold through hatcheries. Breeds that were once naturally broody are now very rarely broody, because many hatcheries have bred the chickens only for their egg production, not for their overall characteristics.

Allowing a broody hen to hatch her own eggs, or eggs that you've purchased, is one of the most fulfilling experiences you can have as a natural chicken keeper. A broody hen is the most natural way to hatch chicks, period. Let's learn all about this old-time skill, and the lost art of the broody hen.

The Signs of the Broody

No two broodies are created equally, and as with anything in life, there are broody "frauds" as well. Some chickens will sit on a nest just to sit on it. They won't actually "accomplish" anything. They might sit on the nest for a couple of hours, right after they've laid an egg, but it doesn't instantly mean they are broody.

Here are some telltale signs that you have a broody hen in your coop:

- **She's a permanent sitter.** She sits on the nest all day and all night when you leave eggs in the nest. She will not get up to roost in the evening with the other chickens when there are eggs in the nest.

- **She pulls feathers.** If she has feathered her nest and she has no plans to leave, she's probably going broody.

- **She screams at you.** Broodies can be vicious things, and rightfully so. They have the ultimate prize to protect! If you go into the coop to remove her from the nest and she puffs herself up and starts screaming a shrill sound at you, chances are she's ready to be a mama.

- **Broody poop.** If you've had a hen that's been sitting on the nest all day and then gets down to "do her doody," her feces will be excessive and will stink to high heavens. Don't worry, you'll know the difference when you smell it and see it!

- **She lays fairly flat.** While laying hens will lay in the nesting box, broodies tend to lay more flat, making sure they cover all of the eggs.

You see, it's not as simple as a hen sitting on a nest for a few hours. Broodies will be exceptionally devoted to sitting on that nest until those eggs hatch. But you're not in the homestretch just yet. Even though a hen may have all the signs of being a good broody, the real trick to knowing if she'll sit on the eggs for the next 21 days is if she continues sitting once you move her.

Will She Still Lay Eggs?

When a hen goes broody, she stops laying eggs. This is partially because she is sitting on a nest and doesn't have time to lay eggs. But more importantly, it's because her feed intake dramatically drops, sending a signal to her body to stop producing eggs until she begins taking in feed at a normal rate once again. Continue offering her regular layer rations as needed, but don't be concerned if she's not eating as often.

There is an art to setting up the broody hen's station in order to ensure a successful experience for both you and your hen. Like painting on a canvas, you'll need to know your setup like the back of your hand, because when you're prepared to move her, it has to happen quickly.

Broody Hen Setup

I have successfully allowed broody hens to hatch in my regular chicken coop, right alongside my flock. The transition for the chicks has been easier, and I much prefer it. However, I still section off a portion of the coop in order to protect my broody and the chicks at all times.

We also have a separate broody hen setup away from the chicken coop, and this is what I suggest that you set up if you're hatching with a

broody for the first time. Once you become more experienced, you'll learn the intuition of the broody and can set her up in a space in your coop. We'll go over both.

Separate Broody Setup

We created a little mini-coop out of an old doghouse. It's enough space for one mother hen and her various chicks. You can use just about anything to create this type of setup, as long as the broody is warm and in a semi-dark and quiet space. She'll do a lot of resting during this time, and she needs not to be disturbed.

Things you can use as a separate broody area:

- An old doghouse (protected)
- An enclosed (with sides) pet carrier/dog crate
- A rabbit hutch
- A small, portable chicken coop with run
- An area of your own creation

Whatever you choose, make sure it is protected, has a run area where your broody can get up and do her business, and is away from the other chickens so that they can't steal her nest.

Chicken Coop Broody Setup

This is, by far, my favorite setup—not just for the ease of transition, but also for the ease of farm chores. Because most hens start going broody in their nesting boxes, I have found a way to set off a nesting box in my coop so that the broody can stay broody but the other hens can't get to her. Some days it takes a little more work, but for the most part, it's an extremely efficient setup.

I start by singling out the nesting box with hardware cloth, making it so that the broody can jump down from the box but not get out. This also means that no chickens can get in. I place a small dish of water and feed in with her on the floor below the nesting box. Should she relieve herself on the floor, I can simply scoop it out as I do chores.

Once the chicks are born, the broody will typically move her nest to the floor area, where I'll make a nest for her and move the chicks to the enclosed floor area. She can then jump up into the nesting box should she ever need to.

You've Got 10 Minutes, Missy

Because most broody hens will get off the nest first thing in the morning to eat and drink with the flock, I do open up the broody area and let the hen stretch her legs. Broodies will typically only stay off the nest for about 10 to 15 minutes at a time, and that's when they need to eat, take a dust bath, and get fresh water. This usually happens once in the morning and once in the evening. As I walk around and do my chores, I make a mental note to check in on the nesting box so that I can be sure no other hen is getting in there and ransacking the place, but this isn't usually a problem when everyone is eating all at one time. However, if it is a problem, you may need to move the broody. Otherwise, other hens could come in and kick the eggs out of the nest, causing cracked and crushed eggs. Once broody mama is done, she hops back on the nest, I close it back up, and we're good to go until dinnertime!

Whichever broody area you choose, the most important step is actually setting up the broody hen in this new area. If the environment you've created for her is to her standards, and you transition her to the area well, you should be set!

Steps for Setting Up Your Broody

The most daunting task of them all is setting up your broody. Let's go step-by-step:

1. **Set up your broody area before you set your hen.** Whether it's in the coop or in a separate space, set it up hours in advance before you move her.

2. **Move your broody hen at night when it's dark outside.** And make sure the new broody area is dark as well. Giving your broody hen a good 15 to 18 hours in the dark with her eggs will help her settle nicely into her new area. Otherwise, she's going to go sit on the original nest, and there won't be any eggs in it!

3. **Don't place the feed and water near the nest.** While this might seem like a good idea, setting the food and water outside of the brooder box will create less of a mess. A good broody will get up and eat and drink when she needs to. Placing the feed and water near the nest can disrupt the area when she's naturally pecking and scratching around.

Herbs and Supplements for the Broody

Allowing a hen to hatch her own eggs is one of the most natural things you can accomplish as a natural chicken keeper. It brings to life an old-time skill that our ancestors mastered. As a modern homesteader and herbalist, however, I know that there are other things you can offer to your broody that may not have been so popular a few centuries ago.

Offering your hen herbs and supplements while she's brooding is a great way to keep her healthy and in good spirits. Always keep in mind that most broody hens don't eat a lot and will tend to start losing

weight. This is completely normal. Don't overload her with herbs and supplements that will just go to waste. Also, continue to give her regular layer feed, even though you'll find that she just won't eat it as often.

Nesting Box Herbs

I love offering some natural aromatherapy to my broody hens. While these herbs won't necessarily add any health benefits for the hen, they do have calming aromatic effects in an enclosed area. Try making this mixture to sprinkle into the nesting area of your broody hen, under her eggs and throughout the nest.

Add equal parts of these dried or fresh herbs for a natural broody mama herb mix:
Chamomile, Lavender, Thyme, Lemon Balm, Basil

Digestive Herbs and Feed

Your broody might need a little digestive boost while she's sitting on that nest. Try some of these herbs and supplements to help calm her digestive tract, keep her full, and still give her a good, healthy, raw food diet while she's nesting.

Herbs to consider (dried or fresh):
Dandelion Leaves, Chamomile, Ginger, Peppermint, Oregano, Basil, Garlic, Thyme

Supplements to consider (in moderation):

Chia seeds, Flaxseeds, Mealworms, Scrambled Eggs, Oats (soaked), Cultured Dried Yeast

Besides the herbal treats and supplemental feed, you'll want to make sure you freshen the nest often. If the hen has excreted feces into the nest or around it, clean it up before she's done with her morning and evening breaks.

Hatching the Eggs

Your hen has an automatic timer in her brain when it comes to hatching her own eggs. She can sense when the time draws closer, and you'll notice she's spending more time on the nest than off during breaks. On the final days, when the eggs begin to hatch, she may not get up at all.

You can hatch your own eggs under the broody, or you can purchase eggs from a breeder. Once you know she's broody, place eggs under her that you find suitable for hatching. If they are your own eggs, place them under her and let her have at it.

If you are purchasing hatching eggs, it can take 2 or 3 days for them to arrive. Simply switch out the eggs each day for new eggs so that the embryos don't start to form. Or purchase ceramic eggs to keep on hand for these types of instances. When your new eggs arrive, simply switch them out with the old eggs in the evening after dark.

Don't forget to keep a running tab on how many days your eggs have been under your hen.

Important: If your hatch with a broody is not successful, immediately remove the eggs and allow the broody to have a few days break. Using a broody back-to-back can cause health issues with your hen, and she may even become extremely unhealthy due to lack of nutrition. If possible, give her a week to recoup before placing new eggs under her and allowing her to brood again.

TIP

A Broody Hen and Her Chicks **77**

This is important with hatching eggs not only in an incubator but also under a broody, because you can lose track of time and have a broody hen sitting for much longer than she should be, causing issues with her health.

The Surrogate Broody

You might have a broody hen but you don't want her to hatch eggs. You can "break" the broody by simply collecting eggs on a regular basis to the point where she eventually gets tired of trying to be broody.

You can also swap out the eggs for day-old chicks (that you purchase from your farm store or hatchery) overnight. There's about a 50 percent chance that she will take them, but more often than not, it seems that when placing the chicks under the broody before it gets too light in the morning, she will take them as her own and you can collect the eggs. She'll raise them like she hatched them!

Transitioning the Broody and Chicks into the Flock

Your final step in the successful broody experience is to transition the broody and her chicks into the flock. If you hatched the chicks in the chicken coop, the broody will naturally transition them. But if you separated the broody from the flock, you'll need to give it a week or so before transitioning.

When you're ready, place the broody and her babies into a dog crate or pet carrier in the run each day so that they can get used to the flock, and the flock and get used to them. Follow the steps described in the previous chapter on transitioning chicks to the flock (see page 66), except keep them with their mama hen at all times.

Broody hens provide an amazing experience on the homestead. We could fill books with stories of broodiness, so I encourage you to check out our website (thefewell homestead.com) for more information, especially on how to encourage broodiness in your hens.

Now that you've learned how to successfully hatch and raise chicks every which way, we can turn to the general health aspect of chicken keeping. It's great to know that through every stage of chicken keeping, even the hatching and chick stage, there are natural alternatives and remedies to common situations.

Raising a Healthy Flock

WE OFTEN HEAR THAT CHICKENS are prey animals and fragile, and while this is completely true, this is also where your strength as a natural chicken keeper comes into play.

The best way to raise a healthy flock is to give them natural tools to keep themselves healthy. This includes giving them a proper diet and free choice of herbs and supplements, doing routine checkups and barn checks, and preparing your livestock medicine cabinet ahead of time.

Preventing diseases, sickness, heat exhaustion, frostbite, and injury are key to maintaining a holistic flock. Of course, sometimes you can do everything natural within your power and things still might go wrong. Throughout this section we'll talk about everything you need to know when it comes to raising a healthy flock. From making your own feed to creating your own tinctures and herbal remedies, this section is packed full of herbal information and healthy chicken advice.

CHAPTER

6

FEED AND DIET

When we first got our flock well under way, I remember reaching out to a local, old-time chicken keeper often. I think I blew up her text messages every few hours asking her, "Is this normal?" "Is this the right feed?" "Should I do this?"

Bless her heart, she never once turned me away, though I could hear the exhaustion in her voice at times. She still patiently answered every question I had, and if she didn't know the answer, she'd point me in the right direction, somehow.

She was a traditional chicken keeper (in the commercial sense) and knew her chickens well. But eventually I found myself drifting further and further away from the traditional chicken keeping methods, and yearned for something a bit more "back to the land."

As I evolved as a chicken keeper, I started becoming a little more natural with my methods. For example, pasture raising my chickens became extremely important to me, as did feeding them herbs. But then I discovered things like diatomaceous earth, a natural product made up of tiny aquatic organisms called diatoms that help with parasites and the digestive tract, and I even started making my own water infusions and decoctions with herbs for our chicken waterers.

Naturally maintaining a healthy flock isn't as hard as one may think. By offering them a natural diet, herbs, and several other supplement and feed options, you can have one of the healthiest flocks around.

What Not to Feed Chickens

While chickens can eat a lot of things, let's list a few things that they shouldn't eat:

- Green potatoes or peels
- Rhubarb
- Avocado pits and skin (we'll touch on this later)
- Black nightshade (*Solanum nigrum*)
- Dried beans (sprouted beans are fine)
- Oleander (*Nerium oleander*)
- Poison hemlock
- Pokeberry (also known as pokeweed)
- Junk food (candy, chocolate, unhealthy restaurant leftovers)
- Moldy foods

Various Ways to Feed Chickens

I know I might get the chicken police after me for this one, but contrary to popular, commercialized opinion . . . you don't have to feed your chickens *only* a layer ration. But if you choose to do so, make sure you choose a non-GMO or organic feed with a minimum of 15 percent protein.

I also like to look for layer feeds that have veggies and whole grains listed first in the ingredients on the back of the package.

(Remember, ingredients on packages list the main ingredient first, and then descend from there.) Thankfully, our local farm co-op mills their own non-GMO chicken feed, which our chickens thoroughly enjoy.

You can purchase commercial brands as well, and while I could spend time naming some of our favorites, these brands might no longer be in production a few years from now. So for this reason I'll just tell you to find a good, wholesome brand of feed that works for you and your flock, and then start implementing other methods in this section . . . if you choose to feed a layer ration at all.

There are a few different ways you can feed your chickens, and you can integrate these with the layer ration, or you can attempt a completely permaculture environment where you feed your chickens strictly from raw feed and pasture. Let's not forget the landrace breeds we mentioned in Chapter 2. These breeds survived centuries on doing what chickens do best—foraging wild food.

WAYS TO FEED CHICKENS

Here are a few options:

- Pasture-raise or raw feed (rotational grazing, free-ranging, feed scraps)
- Make your own feed
- Soak or ferment your feed
- Sprout grains
- Grow fodder
- Feed from compost piles

Encourage Pasture Ranging

People always give me a weird look when I tell them I train my chickens to free-range first, and then eat their feed second (if they eat it at all). But believe it or not, any chicken can be encouraged to wildly forage for its own food, unless there's a

foot of snow on the ground. It's instinctual for any wild bird to forage for its food. Just try to stop a chicken from scratching and pecking at the ground—you can't. It's impossible.

If you're offering a free smorgasbord of grains and feed to your chickens, they most likely won't be encouraged to go find their own food. But then there are some chickens that are always hungry—let's be honest here.

For this very reason, we encourage our chickens to forage for as much of their food as possible, while still giving them the perfect ration of feed. This is one of the main reasons our chicks are on the ground at a week old, or sooner, to mimic what chickens do in nature as much, and as safely, as possible.

As our chickens grow into mature birds, they are encouraged to forage first, then eat their feed last. In fact, before they are even offered feed during the day, they are offered healthy kitchen scraps, compost, fodder, sprouts, and fermented hay or silage. Egg production has never dropped. Our chickens are fat and sassy—and I'm pretty sure they are extra happy as well!

During the growing season, many homesteaders completely free-range their flocks and don't buy feed for six months or more. For example, Karl Hammer of Vermont Compost feeds over 600 chickens completely off his composting systems. I remember reading about him in several articles online, and even in Harvey Ussery's book *The Small-Scale Poultry Flock*. In his 2017 *The Great American Farm Tour* documentary,

Justin Rhodes visited Karl's farm and showed us exactly how Karl feeds all of these chickens strictly on enormous mounds of compost. And we can do exactly that in the backyard and on our homesteads as well—on a small or large scale.

Healthy Kitchen Scraps for Chickens

Imperfect vegetables (raw or cooked, but preferably raw)

Vegetable waste (like the stems and seeds of peppers, cut ends of squash, etc.)

Cooked beans and rice

Fermented vegetables

Kombucha scoby

Water and milk kefir grains (in moderation)

Raw milk (in moderation)

Cultured yogurt (in moderation)

Many backyard gardeners, and even large-scale homesteaders, keep compost piles on their property. Rotating these piles and allowing your chickens to do the "mixing" for you will not only benefit you as the gardener, but also benefit you as the chicken keeper as well. Allowing your chickens to mix your compost also allows them to naturally forage for bugs and food scraps, while ingesting beneficial bacteria from the decomposition of the compost pile.

The bedding and chicken poop from your coop goes into the compost pile, along with feed scraps, organic matter (like leaves), other manure, and more. Your chickens mix the compost pile for you, feeding off of the decomposing future "black gold." And while doing so, they are also depositing more droppings and aerating the compost bed, speeding up the process.

Once fully decomposed and processed, your compost pile will have been almost completely chicken-maintained and ready for you to use. Talk about encouraging foraging, huh? That forage is worth encouraging!

Don't Blend the Treats!

While there are lots of foods you can offer your chickens, you should be wary of some. I'm a firm believer that when given options, chickens will only eat what they want and can eat. For this reason, I never offer my chickens food scraps that have been blended, juiced, or mixed together. I offer them food items that are easy to navigate by sight. For example, many people claim that chickens shouldn't eat the skins and pits of avocados, and while that's true, I've never actually seen a chicken eat the skin or pit of an avocado. I toss old avocados outside and watch as my chickens naturally navigate the bright green fleshy fruit. If I blended that entire avocado, skin and all, I'd likely kill them.

Making Your Own Feed

Many chicken keepers might be interested to know that a natural alternative to commercial layer feed is to make your very own non-GMO or organic chicken feed. Besides

the fact that it is pleasing to the eye with its vibrant grains and veggies (versus compressed pellets), it's also fairly easy to mix together, will last longer (since you'll be using whole grains instead of crushed), and is quite easy to increase and decrease supplements and minerals as you see fit.

There are a few things to consider when making your own feed, such as what vitamins, minerals, and protein you should include.

WHAT DOES MY CHICKEN NEED?

The following vitamins, minerals, and protein are very important in a chicken's diet when giving them strictly feed with little free-ranging or raw feed. Homemade feed is loved by the pasture-ranging chicken keeper and the backyard confined-flock chicken keeper alike.

VITAMINS	MINERALS	PROTEIN
Vitamin A	Calcium	15% to 18% protein intake
Vitamin D	Phosphorous	
Vitamin E	Magnesium	
Vitamin K	Manganese	
Thiamine (B1)	Iron	
Riboflavin (B2)	Copper	
Vitamin B12	Iodine	
Folic Acid	Zinc	
Biotin	Cobalt	
Pantothenic Acid		
Choline		

While this list may look extensive, there are natural mixes, supplements, and other ways to get all of the nutritional benefits of a commercial layer feed. More likely than not, you'll also be able to outsource ingredients from non-GMO or organic sources. Keep in mind that much of the vitamins and minerals will already be included in the main base of your feed, not just in the supplements.

Main Ingredients

There are a few main ingredients that your homemade chicken feed can have. Most chicken feed recipes start out with the same base ingredients, and then add supplements and other items from there. Once you have your base ingredient list down, you can add whatever you see fit for your flock's needs.

Here are some base ingredients to start off with:

1. Wheat
2. Cracked corn
3. Peas (split or whole)
4. Oats (optional; do not feed in excess of 15 percent, as they can cause runny droppings)

Several secondary ingredients are needed as well. Let's break down each one.

Vitamins

You can purchase premixed vitamins for livestock, or you can supplement your chickens' feed with natural raw food sources, like vibrant veggies, and their regular nutritional ingredients (wheat, peas, flax, etc.). You'll find that most of the ingredients I give you in this section already come packed full of most of the vitamins and minerals that chickens need. But adding raw vegetables, like sweet potatoes, carrots, kale, and other vibrant veggies, will increase those vitamins dramatically. You can also do the premixed options if you prefer. Adding cultured dried yeast will also boost the vitamins in the chickens' diet.

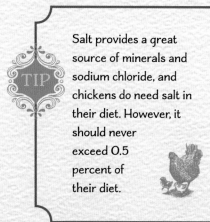

TIP

Salt provides a great source of minerals and sodium chloride, and chickens do need salt in their diet. However, it should never exceed 0.5 percent of their diet.

Minerals

If you're concerned greatly with mineral intake, I suggest purchasing a premix of minerals for your homemade feed (organic Nutri-Balancer is a great option). Once again, adding cultured dried yeast (or brewer's yeast) will also give an exceptional boost of minerals to the chickens' diet. More than anything, however, adding sea kelp to your homemade feed will be your top source of minerals if you're not purchasing a premix.

Protein and Calcium

Feeding crushed eggshells (1 to 4 mm in diameter, not powdered) and oyster shells to your chickens will help with their protein and calcium intake. This is the most popular way to boost these nutritional needs. You can offer these free choice or mix them into your feed, but I prefer to offer free choice. Chickens take in what they need when it comes to protein and calcium, and generally consume it in the evenings so that their bodies slowly absorb it while they roost. Fish meal is a great option to increase both protein and calcium intake as well. Just try not to exceed 5 percent of the chickens' diet with fish meal, otherwise your eggs will taste fishy! Not only is it great for protein and calcium, but it also efficiently boosts omega-3 fatty acids in egg yolks. Aragonite and limestone are two other great options to boost calcium intake as well.

Good Bacteria

We know that allowing chickens to mix our compost piles is beneficial when it comes to taking in good bacteria, but if that's not an option for you, you might consider adding good bacteria to your homemade feed. You can do this by adding probiotics or direct-fed microbials, which can be bought prepackaged. These ingredients help maintain a healthy digestive tract for your chickens. In case you haven't caught on yet, I also highly recommend adding cultured dried yeast (or brewer's yeast) to your homemade feed. This not only offers live-cell yeast cultures that enhance digestion, but also gives your chickens a fantastic boost in vitamins and minerals.

Add Raw Apple Cider Vinegar!

Adding raw organic apple cider vinegar (ACV) to your chicken's waterer or feed every day will help keep their bodies alkaline (instead of acidic) and will keep good bacteria flowing throughout their digestive tract. Add 1 tablespoon to a gallon waterer, or spray their food down (daily, in the scoop) with ACV before offering it to them. You can do this daily or every other day.

Finishing Your Mix

Now that you know what ingredients you need other than your main players, let's go over what to add to your base feed.

TIP Mix up your vitamins, minerals, and supplements in a container and simply sprinkle the mixture into your chicken's daily feed scoop instead of mixing it into their feed bin when you make the original batch of feed. Only make small batches of supplements at a time so that they don't go bad as quickly.

VITAMINS, MINERALS, AND SUPPLEMENTS:

Sea kelp

Black oil sunflower seeds

Cultured dry yeast

Flaxseed

Calcium source (eggshells, aragonite, or oyster shells; grit)

Fish meal (optional)

Next you add your premixes of minerals or vitamins, remembering that your chickens are already getting minerals and vitamins from some of the ingredients listed here. Don't overthink it!

In order to ensure your layers are getting at least 15 percent protein, make sure you're offering at least 6 percent as calcium ingredients (like aragonite, fish meal, or a mixed source) in your feed. You can use your premixes to attain the 15 percent protein, as it will be labeled on the back of the mix's packaging. Keeping in mind that 15 percent is the minimum, it's fine to go up from there.

Basic Natural Chicken Feed Recipe

Based on 100 pounds of feed*

Wheat (20 to 25 pounds)

Cracked corn (20 to 25 pounds)

Peas, split or whole (20 to 25 pounds)

Oats (optional; do not feed in excess of 15 percent, as they can cause runny droppings)

Black oil sunflower seeds (5 pounds)

Flaxseed (1 pound; do not exceed 10 percent)

Mineral premix (optional; 0.5 to 2 pounds, depending on pasture availability)

Free choice:

> Sea kelp
>
> Grit
>
> Cultured dry yeast
>
> Fish meal (optional; not to exceed 5 percent)
>
> Calcium source (eggshells, aragonite, or oyster shells)

*Slight flexibility has been given in the base portion of this recipe so that you can adjust according to your needs if you pasture-range. Birds that are on pasture generally get more vitamins and nutrients than those in confinement.

Making your own feed is a fabulous natural option if you're trying to get away from commercial layer pellets, and even if you're pasture ranging and need a wholesome feed for the winter months.

There are other, more natural ways to supplement feed, though. Let's look at the other options!

Don't forget, grit is especially necessary for chickens that aren't on pasture or free-ranging. It helps the gizzard break up grains and feed! You can purchase grit, or even just grab a handful of sand near a creek bed to throw in with your chickens. Grit consists of small pebbles, sand, and other natural gritty substances from the earth.

Soaking Your Chicken Feed for Easy Digestion

Not only do human bodies digest grains better when they have been soaked or fermented, but so do chickens and other livestock. The act of soaking or fermenting grains breaks down the grain, causing it to become a better nutrient that is more easily absorbed into the body. Soaking and fermenting your chicken feed, especially your homemade feed, is beneficial to the overall health of your chicken flock and encourages good bacteria throughout their intestinal tracts. It also helps your chickens absorb the good vitamins and minerals that you're giving them. As with most things in chicken keeping, it's very simple to incorporate soaked feed into your daily routine.

How to Soak Chicken Feed

For this routine, you'll simply need to keep two 5-gallon food-grade buckets on hand. All you'll need is feed and water.

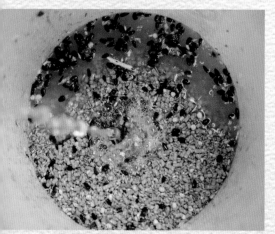

Step 1: Depending on your flock size, put half the amount of feed that you normally give your flock into a 5-gallon bucket. For a flock of twelve, start with one-half to one scoop of feed. Cover with fresh water (non-chlorinated), just enough to get all of the feed soaked but leaving about 4 inches of water over the grains. Keep in mind the grains will swell as they soak up the water, which is why we need the extra water on top. It's best to do this step in the morning so

that it's ready to feed by the following morning. Allow the feed to sit in the bucket, covered loosely, and soak for 24 hours.

Step 2: The next morning, inspect the feed to make sure that all looks okay. If there is an excessive amount of water left, you've added too much water and should just pour it off. Make a mental note of this with the next batch you make and adjust accordingly. Offer the soaked feed to your chickens, and watch them chow down!

Step 3: Mix a new batch of soaked feed to be ready for the following morning. *That's it!*

It's important to keep track of what your chickens are eating. Typically, with soaked feed, you'll find your chickens eat less feed, or *need* less feed since the nutritional value is higher. But pay attention to your flock and adjust as needed.

Fermenting Chicken Feed

Fermenting chicken feed seems to be an increasingly popular practice in the twenty-first century, but we don't typically practice it on our homestead. Besides the fact that it takes up a lot of room in the kitchen pantry or on the counter—and the squirrels have a field day with it if we leave it outside—we are able to attain a lot of the same benefits as fermented feed by making our own feed, soaking it, adding activated cultures to it, offering beneficial herbs, and pasture raising. That said, fermenting feed is certainly a fun experiment, and I encourage you to pursue it if you're interested!

Here's a quick and easy way to ferment your chicken feed:

Step 1: Start with a whole-grain feed mix. Using processed pellets or crumbles generally doesn't work well.

Step 2: Fill up a 1-gallon glass jar or food-grade bucket about three-fourths of the way with feed. Cover the feed completely with non-chlorinated water, leaving about 4 inches of water above the feed. Cover the top of the jar or bucket lightly with a cloth.

Step 3: Allow the mixture to sit for a few days indoors out of direct sunlight, stirring once or twice each day and adding water as needed. The feed should be covered at all times with water.

Step 4: After a few days, you'll begin to see bubbles on top of and rising from the mixture. This means that lacto-fermentation has started. You can feed this to your chickens immediately, or you can allow it to sit for another day or two for an even richer fermented feed. Keep in mind that you'll offer less feed than a normal scoop, because fermented feed is more easily digestible and better absorbed by your chicken's digestive tract.

Try offsetting batches of feed so that you have feed fermenting at all times rather than having to start a brand-new batch each time you feed your old batch. On day 1 make your first batch, on day 2 make a second batch, and so on.

Growing Fodder

When the winter months are long and you are craving a hint of green to appear in the yard once again, chances are your chickens are craving as well. One of the best ways to provide your chickens with lush, green grass is to grow your own. Whether it's because there's a foot of snow on the ground or because you simply don't have the ability or setup for your chickens to free-range, growing your own fodder is a great alternative to pasture.

You'll want to start with a reliable organic source for wheatgrass or pasture grass. Many options can be found online, and sometimes can even be bought in bulk at your local farm store.

Here are a few types of grains you can grow or sprout:

Wheat

Oats

Barley

Rye

Wheat has the highest protein content, while barley and oats have the most digestible fiber content. A higher starch content is found in wheat and rye, while barley and oats have lower values. Barley, by far, has the highest calcium percentage. Keep all of these things in mind when choosing a grain for your flock or mixing several grains together.

All grains become 40 percent more digestible when sprouted or grown into fodder. For this reason, your chickens will need to consume less fodder than their regular feed ration because not only is the nutritional value higher, but the absorption rate into the chicken's system is greater as well.

Chickens need 2 to 3 percent of their body weight in fodder each day, if you're feeding them only fodder daily. Offer it along with grit and mineral and vitamin supplements.

How to Grow Fodder

You can grow fodder in as small or as large a batch as you like. Since we don't use it as a full-time feed on our homestead, I simply grow it in my little greenhouse in the winter months or on the kitchen table, when necessary. But if you want to supplement feed with fodder, you'll need to set up an entire system.

What you'll need:

Shallow container (I use old plastic or metal cake pans)

Grain of choice

Water (non-chlorinated)

Step 1: Soak the grains in a food-grade bucket or bowl overnight. This will jumpstart the process.

Step 2: Find a sturdy shallow container, preferably something you can drill holes into, as the base for your fodder. Old plastic or metal cake pans work well. Drill lots of little holes in the bottom—big enough to allow water to drain through, but small enough so that the grains don't escape. You may have to place a plastic mesh liner in the bottom of the pan if your holes are too big.

Step 3: Add your soaked grains to the pan, no more than 2 inches thick. I like to add just a thin layer, until I can't see the bottom of the pan any longer.

Step 4: Keep the grains moist, but not soaked, until they begin to sprout. You can do this by using a water-filled spray bottle or by simply running the fodder under water each day and allowing it to drain fully.

Step 5: After 3 to 7 days, your fodder will be sprouting nicely, depending on the temperature where the fodder is located. Once the fodder reaches the desired height, flip it upside down onto a clean surface and cut from the bottom, where the roots are. Make 4-inch squares, or whatever size you desire, and offer them to your chickens as needed!

Fodder can take a few tries to master, but once you've mastered it, you'll begin putting together a rotational system that suits your needs.

While fodder is great, putting your chickens on pasture most of the year is the best option, if your space allows. Fodder acts as a pasture replacement when pasture raising isn't an option or isn't available during cold months.

Rotational Grazing Your Chickens

Chicken keeper and author Joel Salatin brought one of the most revolutionary practices in the chicken industry to the spotlight. It's called "rotational grazing," and it's one of the best options for the natural chicken keeper. Of course, not everyone has the option to pasture raise or rotational graze due to space limitations. In fact, most modern homesteaders and back-yard chicken keepers live on an acre or less. However, even in small spaces, rotational grazing is absolutely attainable depending on your flock size.

Don't have time or space to make fodder? Try sprouting wheat, broccoli, peas, or other grains and veggies in a mason jar. Simply soak them every day in water, drain well, and watch them grow!

TIP

If you're starting from scratch, you'll want to make sure that your pasture is well established. If you need to reseed grass with a pasture mix, and even with herbs, do so in the early spring before the ground gets too warm, or in the fall for a spring growth. Cover your seed with a very light layer of straw. You can add manure, compost, or fertilizer too if you'd like. A little goes a long way.

Over the next few weeks, you'll see your grass taking hold and growing quickly. Once your pasture has reached a desirable stage, you can start with your rotational grazing.

The goal is to offer at least three or four different paddocks for your chickens to pasture in, allowing at least 2 weeks (preferably 4 weeks) before starting the rotation all over again. In larger spaces, allowing 30 days between starting on paddock number one all over again is ideal, but for smaller spaces, allowing at least 2 weeks is a big help.

If you have a larger field with pasture-ranging setups in movable chicken tractors, you can easily rotate your flocks (meat birds *and* layers) on a daily basis, never having them touch the same space twice in a 30- to 60-plus-day period.

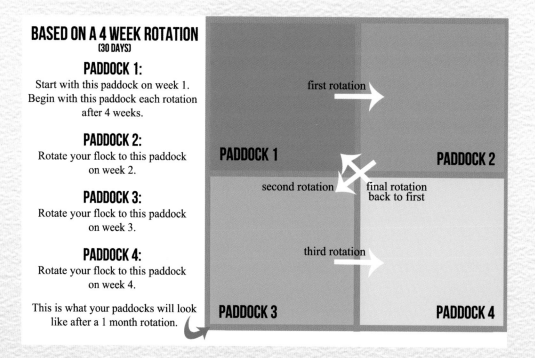

BASED ON A 4 WEEK ROTATION
(30 DAYS)

PADDOCK 1:
Start with this paddock on week 1. Begin with this paddock each rotation after 4 weeks.

PADDOCK 2:
Rotate your flock to this paddock on week 2.

PADDOCK 3:
Rotate your flock to this paddock on week 3.

PADDOCK 4:
Rotate your flock to this paddock on week 4.

This is what your paddocks will look like after a 1 month rotation.

first rotation

PADDOCK 1

PADDOCK 2

second rotation   final rotation back to first

third rotation

PADDOCK 3

PADDOCK 4

Not only does rotational grazing allow the grass to root deeply into the ground, therefore creating a much more fertile pasture, but it is also healthier for your chickens to be on a rotational grazing system.

Here's why rotational grazing is natural and beneficial to your flock and your land:

There are fewer parasites. Your chickens will be far less likely to contract internal and external parasites when rotationally grazing. This is due to the fact that they are not constantly in contact with their feces, other animals' feces, or the soil that they are walking on. Rotation allows the parasites in feces and in the ground to die off or dissipate since they don't have a host to inhabit. This means that your chances of getting parasites (like worms) and bacteria (like coccidiosis) are drastically reduced.

It increases forage production. Rotational grazing can increase foraging production by 30 to 70 percent due to the fact that you aren't overgrazing and killing the pasture. More fertility for the soil and the chickens!

You can use your chickens to till and clean. Think outside of the box! Instead of just rotating chickens on grass and pasture, rotate them into your garden areas as well. Put your chickens in your garden area in the winter so that they till it up and fertilize it all winter long. When spring comes, place them back out on pasture to forage freely, and start back up with weekly rotations. If you have large livestock, like cows or sheep, you can rotate your chickens behind your rotation of larger livestock, which allows the chickens to clean up their mess. Picking through cow patties and getting rid of fly larvae and other undesirables, chickens can provide an important service!

A smaller feed bill. Yep, your feed bill will be nonexistent during the most productive foraging seasons. Your chickens will become expert foragers when given the chance and natural opportunity to forage. This will decrease your feed bill substantially.

There are plenty of other benefits to rotationally grazing your animals. The list is really never-ending if we were to get down to the scientific specifics, but I'll spare you the time.

COOPS, CHICKEN MAINTENANCE, AND MORE

There are some things about natural chicken keeping that don't really need an entire chapter devoted to them. I like to call it the "maintenance and common sense" section. In this chapter we'll hit the highs and lows of chicken maintenance and other nuggets of knowledge, like general coop size and spacing.

Most of these things are just plain common sense. As you see a problem arising, you deal with it. But sometimes, we might not know *how* to deal with it. So, let's learn to deal with it!

General Coop Maintenance and Information

There are all kinds of chicken coops, from bright, elaborate, all-white coops with chandeliers and fancy curtains to everyday coops made out of pallets with no bells and whistles. Whatever your preference, make sure you know basic maintenance techniques to ensure happiness for your flock.

The Coop Size

From small coops that only hold two chickens to large barns that can hold hundreds, your coop size will make a world of difference.

As a general rule of thumb, each chicken should have at least 4 square feet of space inside the coop. This guarantees that they can walk about and stretch out their wings without hitting another chicken.

Outside of the coop, I always suggest having double this amount (8 square feet). In fact, I'm a major advocate for wide-open spaces and allowing chickens as much space as they desire. However, I understand some chicken keepers can only raise their chickens in confinement. Use the 4-square-foot rule as a minimum space requirement per bird, then go up from there.

The Roosts

Roosts are platforms or bars in your coop where your chickens sleep at night. Chickens enjoy roosting in high places, as it's instinctually less likely for a predator to grab them in such a high area versus being on the ground. For this reason, we build roosts in our chicken coops.

Purchasing Adult Chickens

If you're purchasing adult chickens, make sure you quarantine them for at least 30 days before introducing them to the rest of your flock. They will need to go through a transition period just as you would transition chicks to a new flock; you can read more about that on page 66. Make sure you have a transition station set up away from your coop.

Your roosts should be higher than your nesting boxes but not directly above them, as you want to avoid having feces fall into the nesting area. Typical roosts are at least 4 to 5 feet tall. You can create tiered roosts so that older or smaller birds can roost on the lower roost if necessary.

Roosts can be as simple as tree branches or 2-by-4 pieces of lumber, or they can be actual platforms that you create with flat pieces of lumber.

The Nesting Boxes

Nesting boxes—the most sacred of all chicken spaces. They're where the action happens, after all! From the egg layer to the broody hen, a

nesting box is one of the most important components of the chicken coop.

Nesting boxes should be at least 12 inches wide, 12 inches deep, and 9 inches tall. Your hens will care more about the width and depth than the height.

Make sure that your nesting boxes are low enough for your chickens to jump into. You can use just about anything for a nesting box if you don't want to build your own. Chances are, your hens are going to find their favorite spots to lay anyhow, and it might just be right on the floor!

Nesting Box Ideas

Want to spruce up your coop? Try using these options rather than building nesting boxes:

- Old wooden or antique crates
- Buckets turned on their sides
- Old milk crates
- Old wine crates
- Old furniture (like bookshelves)
- Barrel planters
- Old shelving or deep book shelves

Your nesting boxes should be clean at all times in order to encourage hens to lay in them. Make sure you're collecting eggs each day and refreshing their bedding as needed. This helps prevent broken eggs or hens being enticed to lay elsewhere due to overcrowding.

The Bedding

Your coop bedding will be your signature as a chicken keeper. I never knew there could be so much controversy around chicken coop bedding, but there most certainly seems to be.

Here's a simple rule of thumb: Choose a bedding that is natural or easy to break down when composted. That is your best option as a natural chicken keeper.

I only use straw, dirty wood chips (not the landscape kind), or cardboard bedding. All of these beddings have proven themselves to be natural and easy to break down when necessary. They are also easy to use with the deep litter method, which we use throughout the year.

You can get the cardboard and straw bedding at your local farm store, though I hear an increasing number of people are having a harder time finding the cardboard chips than the straw.

The Deep Litter Method

I completely clean out my chicken coop thoroughly four times a year as a deep clean. Not having to clean out the bedding more often than that can be accomplished by using the deep litter method. If you have just a few chickens, you may only have to clean out your coop a couple of times each year, but with ten or more chickens, you'll be cleaning it at least three or four times a year.

The deep litter method is simple. Place at least 6 inches of straw or cardboard bedding onto the floor of your coop and turn over the bedding each day. This continuous stirring of the bedding and feces is much like composting. After a few days, your bedding will begin attracting good microbes and bacteria, and it will start to break down. There should never be much of a smell of ammonia, though it will still smell like chickens.

If you don't want to use straw or cardboard, you can use leaves and grass clippings, and continue to stir that each day, once or twice a day, whenever you feed your chickens. You can also sprinkle feed on the floor of your coop and have the chickens turn the bedding over for you!

Never allow the litter to get wet by water or waterers, as this will heighten the chances of bad bacteria, like mold, to begin growing. Remove the litter immediately if this occurs.

A Word on Sand Bedding

While sand bedding has become increasingly popular with chicken keepers, it is much too difficult for me to keep up with. Sand can harbor bacteria and other nasties, and needs to be removed once a year for a good cleaning, allowing the coop and sand to be dried out and to fix any issues with your coop floor. Sand stays wet constantly, and this can encourage bad bacterial growth. This is the number one reason we don't use it.

However, if you choose to use it, I'd encourage you to use a construction-grade sand and keep it meticulously clean, dry, and a safe place for your chickens.

Predator Protection

You put a lot of time and love into your chickens, and when a predator comes along and snatches one (or an entire flock) away from you, it is heartbreaking and frustrating. The photograph above shows just how destructive this can be to your property as well. This photograph was taken on a friend's property when a bear ransacked their entire coop.

Here are some tips to help predator-proof your chicken coop and run:

- Make sure that all of the doors on your coop lock with a twist or slip lock. Many predators, like raccoons, can open simple doors with their little paws.

- If you have a chicken run, bury the wire in the dirt (at least 2 feet deep) so that predators have a hard time digging in.

- While chicken wire was created to keep chickens in, it was not created to keep predators out. In high-predator areas, I always recommend using hardware cloth, rather than chicken wire, for the bottom portion of your chicken run, windows, and other areas where predators could get in.

- Place bird netting over your coop so that sky predators, like hawks, can't swoop down into your run.

- Hang reflective items from trees or install on the ground of your chicken run to deter flying predators.

- Install a motion-detecting light that will come on should a predator walk by. You can purchase predator detection lights or make one of your own.

- Utilize livestock guardian dogs.

Predators

Some of the most common predators you'll notice around your homestead are:

- Sky predators (hawks, eagles, owls, and crows)
- Raccoons
- Possums
- Foxes
- Coyotes
- Weasels
- Rats
- Bears

While it's less common for a bear to attack your chickens, it does happen. More often than not, bears will pry open your chicken coop like a can of tuna when trying to get at your chicken feed. In the process, they will certainly snag a chicken!

These easy tips can help predator-proof your coop and save you from loss in the long run. Predators are swift and abundant, especially once they know where the "food" is. Livestock guardian dogs are your best bet to protect the chickens during the day and night; however, these other steps will help tremendously as well.

Coop Must-Knows

Maintaining chicken coops doesn't have to be difficult. Make sure that your coop is sturdily built and that it has plenty of ventilation, protection against predators, and fresh bedding and clean nesting boxes. Offer these things to your chickens, and you'll have the happiest flock yet!

Here are a few more things to remember when choosing or building your coop:

Ventilation is key. Make sure that there's plenty of it so that your coop is cool in the summer and doesn't hold moisture in the winter. Vents should always be at the top portion of the coop.

Keep the drafts away. Wintertime drafts are the worst. Make sure you board up your coop, or place plastic over open spaces, while still allowing good ventilation in the bitter cold months. Your chickens can't stay warm with wind whipping around them!

Add vinyl or linoleum to the floor. This will help the cleaning process along. If you utilize the deep litter method, you should be able to sweep out the bedding with little effort!

Don't place waterers in the coop. This encourages mold growth and soaking wet floors—neither are a good thing!

No matter what type of coop you choose, or how many chickens you fill it with, the goal is to have fun with it all! Make sure your coop outline has all of these important things, and then create a space that mimics your lifestyle, character, and personalized touch. Paint your walls teal if you want to, it doesn't matter. As long as you love it, that's the best part of having your own coop!

CHAPTER

8

USING HERBS IN FEED
AND ON PASTURE

Animals have been foraging for wild and common herbs on their own since the beginning of time. I am constantly amazed at the exuberance we humans show when we offer herbs to our animals, as if this is some type of new trend. Given the chance, your chickens would naturally forage for their own herbs on an as-needed basis. This is why, as a holistic chicken keeper, I enjoy offering herbs to them not only in the feed I make, but also around the areas where my chickens roam freely.

I like to offer my flock homemade herb mixes on a regular basis. You can combine the herb mix with their daily feed ration (as we talked about previously), or you can simply toss a handful out every day as you'd like to. If you're feeling extra adventurous, you can landscape your property with perennial and wild herbs or plant a pasture grass (if your chickens free-range) with wild and common herbs mixed in wherever your flocks roam.

I firmly believe that when chickens eat herbs on a regular basis as part of their daily or weekly diet, it can help prevent many illnesses and parasites, just as it does with humans. We've found this to be true in our own flocks over the years, and within our own bodies.

Not only is it healthy for your chickens, but it's healthy for you as well. There are many ways to naturally enhance the nutritional value of those glorious eggs that you eat for breakfast every morning, and we do this by offering herbs and wild edibles. Many of the herbs and edibles that I mention in this list are packed full of vitamins and minerals, and even omega-3 fatty acids. If you're looking to avoid adding pre-mixed store-bought minerals and vitamins to your homemade chicken feed, this is a great chapter to study up on for various natural and wild options.

Here are my favorite herbs that you can add to your chicken feed and why they are important, followed by a general herb mix recipe. You don't need to put *all* of the herbs in the feed, unless you want to. I would suggest a base recipe, and then tailor it to your flock's specific needs moving forward with additions. Also, keep in mind that when we reach the ailments chapter of this book, there are other herbs mentioned that aren't on this list. These are simply the herbs we keep on hand at all times for feed and common needs.

The Herb List

Astragalus (Astragalus membranaceus)

Most commonly known for its immune-stimulating properties, astragalus is one of the most beneficial herbs you can offer to your chickens on a regular basis as a preventative herb. In fact, a study done in 2013 showed that astragalus helped prevent avian influenza and shortened the duration of the flu as well. While the study primarily focused on the injection of astragalus, as an herbalist, I know that astragalus as a dietary supplement stimulates the immune system greatly, thus very likely preventing the inhabitation of the influenza virus. Besides avian influenza, astragalus helps boost the overall immune system of the chicken, generating good health and wellness. It is also anti-inflammatory, helps chickens adapt to stress, and is antibacterial and antiviral.

Dosage: Give to your chickens a couple times each week to boost their immune systems, either dried or in a decoction (see page 125). I prefer to offer it in a decoction, and my chickens prefer it that way as well.

Basil (Ocimum basilicum)

Basil is a great herb that many people can grow right in a windowsill. When given to chickens, it helps support a healthy immune system, respiratory system, and digestive tract, and is even anti-inflammatory. Basil is full of rich antioxidants that are necessary for your chooks' bodies to stay healthy and stress-free.

Dosage: You can offer this free choice or in feed daily, or as needed.

Calendula (Calendula officinalis)

Many chicken keepers think that any marigold is a calendula plant, but that's just not true. Make sure that you're adding *Calendula officinalis* to your feed when using calendula. This herb is a natural anti-inflammatory and helps the digestive tract. But more importantly, it is packed full of omega-3s, vitamins E and K, and B-complex vitamins. This means that your egg yolks will come out with a deep, rich orange color, full of necessary nutrients and omega-3s for your *own* body!

Dosage: You can offer this free choice or in feed daily.

Chamomile (Matricaria recutita)

This is one of my favorite herbs of all time. It smells incredible and is delicious. Chamomile aids in digestion, helps heal mucous membranes, is anti-inflammatory and antispasmodic, and can act as a mild sedative. Chamomile is best used only in times of stress or as a random treat when respiratory or digestive aid is needed.

Dosage: Offer chamomile after a predator attack, a time when your flock is stressed, or to a broody hen.

Chickweed (Stellaria media)

Most chicken keepers have this wild herb growing around their backyard. You can find this creeping plant growing just about anywhere, and your chickens will love it! Chickweed helps support the digestive tract and respiratory system, and is high in vitamins C, A, D, and B—though most notably for C. It also offers a great dose of daily iron, calcium, and potassium.

Dosage: Offer daily in season, or plant on pasture where chickens roam freely.

Comfrey (Symphytum spp.)

Comfrey is one of the kings in the herb community. In fact, it has most often been a substitute for feed in certain farming methods. While I don't suggest completely replacing your feed with comfrey (as there are some toxicity concerns), it is full of vitamins and minerals that are beneficial to your chickens. Comfrey is high in vitamins A, C, and B_{12} and is also high in protein. Its leaves contain calcium, potassium, phosphorus, and some iron. Comfrey can reduce pain, is anti-inflammatory, boosts the immune system, and supports bones.

Dosage: Offer once a week or so in small batches (several fresh leaves each week), or plant a few comfrey plants on pasture. These plants can be invasive, so be careful with placement.

Dandelion (Taraxacom officinale)

Don't kill those beautiful little dandelions that pop up in the yard. Instead, pick them for your chickens or allow your chickens to free-range where the dandelions are! Dandelions are high in vitamins A, B_6, C, and K and are also full of calcium and fiber. They support bone and heart health and are high in antioxidants, and dandelion greens are a great source of omega-3s!

Dosage: Offer freely as you wish in season, or plant on pasture where chickens roam freely.

Echinacea (Echinacea purpurea or Echinacea angustifolia)

One of the most common herbs to the new herbalist, the roots, leaves, and flower heads of the echinacea plant are immune boosters. I toss the leaves and the flower heads to the chickens and allow them free choice. This herb is also great for the respiratory system and can help

treat fungal overgrowth. It is also a natural antibiotic and is naturally antibacterial.

Dosage: Offer freely as you wish in season, or dry and offer throughout the year.

Garlic (Allium sativum)

Garlic, in my opinion, is one of the easiest herbs to grow for your chickens. But if you can't grow it yourself, it's also readily available at the grocery store. Add dried minced garlic to feed or whole smashed cloves a few times a week to their water or herb mix. Garlic stimulates the digestive tract, regulates liver function, boosts the immune system, and fights and treats infections, since it is a natural antibacterial. It's also thought to help deworm chickens and other livestock.

Dosage: Offer daily in feed or ration, or a couple of times each week in an herb mix.

Lamb's-Quarter (Chenopodium album)

This wild herb is packed full of vitamins A, C, B_1, and B_2, as well as iron and protein. While it doesn't hold much medicinal value, other than supporting a healthy digestive tract, it is a fabulous wild herb that is full of nutrients for your flock.

Dosage: Feed daily in season or plant on pasture (or allow to grow on pasture, since it's wild).

Lemon Balm (Melissa officinalis)

Lemon balm grows wild and free in most places

and smells exactly like fresh lemon—hence its name. This herb spreads like wildfire, since it's part of the mint family, so you'll always have enough of it to spare for your chooks. Lemon balm aids in digestion, is a natural antioxidant, calms the nervous system, is antiviral and antibacterial, and promotes fertility. It's also thought to help deworm chickens and other livestock. Dosage: I like to use lemon balm all year long and feed it fresh daily in with the feed ration, by the handful, or dried throughout the year in my herb mix.

Mint (Peppermint or Spearmint)

Both peppermint and spearmint are great options for your chickens. They are antiseptic, aid in digestive and respiratory health, and are a natural painkiller. I like to grow peppermint patches and allow the chickens to forage through them once they are mature. Once they've weeded through the patch a bit, I take them out of that foraging area and allow the mint to grow back up. Each time I'll harvest a bit in season and dry it so that I have enough on hand during the wintertime, when respiratory issues could come up.

Nasturtium (Tropaeolaceae)

This cute little plant is a powerhouse antibacterial and has strong antibiotic and antimicrobial properties. Nasturtium is also high in vitamin

C, which helps boost the immune system. It may be helpful during the deworming or preventative worming of your chickens.

Dosage: Give freely when in season or dried out of season. Plant around your chicken run or in your pasture where the nasturtiums can climb.

Oregano (Origanum vulgare)

Oregano is growing in popularity, not just with the backyard chicken keeper but with commercial chicken keepers as well. In fact, many large commercial meat and egg producers have switched to offering oregano and thyme in their chicken feed on a regular basis instead of chemicals and antibiotics. Oregano is a natural antibiotic, is antibacterial, detoxifies the body, aids in respiratory health, and helps the reproductive system.

Dosage: Mix in with your chicken feed daily, fresh or dried, or infuse in waterers.

Plantain (Plantago lanceolata)

Chickens love this wild edible, and it normally grows in abundance. It is a natural anti-inflammatory, soothes the respiratory tract, protects the liver, and is full of vitamins and minerals. Plantain contains fiber, potassium, calcium, magnesium, sodium, phosphorus, zinc, and copper, as well as vitamins A, C, and K. It is also high in antioxidants. This is one wild herb that I allow to grow freely in my garden and yard. It is a great wild edible to grow on pasture as well.

Dosage: Offer it daily, or as you deem necessary, when in season.

Purple Dead Nettle (Lamium purpureum)

This wild herb pops up all across the landscape when spring arrives. While part of the nettle family, it is not like stinging nettle—no sting on this wild one! However, it is a natural antibacterial, anti-inflammatory, and antifungal herb. Dosage: Pluck from the yard for a delicious and nutritious treat for your flock when in season, or grow on pasture.

Purslane (Portulaca oleracea)

Not only is purslane one of my favorite herbs for the homestead, but it has also come to be one of the most necessary wild herbs for my chicken flock. This wild edible is a no-brainer for your chickens. Purslane contains more omega-3 fatty acids than many fish oil supplements. Many commercial egg companies take pride in offering eggs that are packed full of omega-3s, and there's a good reason why: They're healthier for you! You'd be surprised how many people have an omega-3 deficiency. In addition to omega-3s, purslane is high in vitamins A and C and B-complex vitamins, plus minerals such as iron, magnesium, calcium, potassium, and manganese. It is an incredible source of natural antioxidants.

Dosage: Offer freely when in season; plant on pasture. Harvest when in season, dry, and add to your chicken feed throughout the year for a natural boost in vitamins and minerals.

Red Clover (*Trifolium pratense*)

Another wild edible, this herb specifically helps support fertility and the reproductive system. Red clover has been planted in pastures and used for livestock feed for centuries. It is a great cover crop.

Dosage: Offer on pasture daily when in season, or weekly dried.

Rosemary (*Rosmarinus officinalis*)

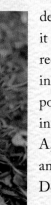

An aromatic herb in every homesteader's garden, rosemary enhances brain function (though it probably won't make your chickens smarter!), reduces stress, promotes liver function, aids in digestion, and improves circulation. It is a powerhouse antioxidant and a natural anti-inflammatory and is a good source of vitamins A, C, and B_6, as well as folate, calcium, iron, and manganese.

Dosage: Offer weekly in herb mix, or plant around pasture and chicken run for free-choice herbing.

Sage (*Salvia officinalis*)

We often think of sage when cooking homestead dishes, but it is also a great herb for your chickens. Most importantly, it helps treat viral and fungal infections, and helps prevent them, too. It also aids in digestion. Sage is rich in vitamins A and C and B-complex vitamins and is also a great source of beta-carotene.

Dosage: Offer weekly in herb mix, or plant around pasture and chicken run for free-choice herbing.

Stinging Nettle (Urtica dioica)

Chickens won't typically touch this herb in its natural environment, though some flocks will. Stinging nettle does exactly what it says it does—it stings. The little hairs on the outside of the leaves can cause a numbing sensation for many humans and animals. However, sting-ing nettle is an incredible source of vitamins,

nutrients, and minerals for your chickens. Try giving it to them fresh first to see if they will eat it. If not, you may have to cook it down, like spinach, or dry it out first. Stinging nettle is a natural detoxifier and antiparasitic, and aids in respiratory health. It is also a natural antibacterial. Throughout history, many chicken keepers have offered stinging nettles to their chickens and sworn that it keeps them laying straight through the entire year. Nettle is also naturally high in iron and calcium. Wild birds will eat stinging nettle as a way to help prevent internal parasites, and chickens will absolutely do the same thing. Nettles are a great way to prevent internal parasites and possibly treat an infesta-tion when given in medicinal doses.

Dosage: Give freely throughout the year—fresh, dried, or cooked—or a couple of offerings each week.

Thyme (Thymus vulgaris)

Thyme is my all-time favorite herb. We use it with every single animal on our homestead.

Thyme is a natural antiparasitic and antibacterial, aids the respiratory system, relieves infection, and is packed full of omega-3s that support brain and heart health. It is also rich in vitamins A, C, and B6, as well as fiber, iron, riboflavin, manganese, and calcium.

Dosage: Offer daily in their feed, dried or fresh, or freely on pasture or around the chicken run.

Herbs on Pasture

You've heard of something being "on tap" (i.e., always available). Well, "herbs on pasture" is exactly like that—herbs on tap! You can make a mix of perennial herb seeds and pasture grass for your own backyard or pasture. Simply start with a good pasture grass mix, then add your wild or common herb seeds. Make sure you get perennials that will come back bigger and stronger each year for your flock.

This process will allow your flock to add herbs to their diet as they free-range, and even gives them the option to self-medicate when needed!

Herbs to consider for your pasture:

Oregano	Purslane
Thyme	Red clover
Plantain	Mint
Chickweed	Lemon balm
Wild violet	Lamb's-quarter
Rosemary	Purple dead nettle

While this herb and wild edibles list is extensive, you can put together a basic herb mix and then add random herbs as your flock needs them, or whenever they are in season. Here is my base recipe that I add to my chicken's feed each day or a couple

of times a week. I mix up a large batch that can
last about one month at a time. You don't want
opened containers of herbs lying around too
long, otherwise they begin to lose their efficacy.

BASIC HERB MIX (DRIED)

Equal parts:
Thyme
Oregano
Echinacea
Garlic
Lemon balm
Stinging nettle

Add 1 cup of basic herb mix to your flock's daily ration, or add several times
each week.

Making Water Infusions and Decoctions

Herbs in your flock's diet aren't always necessary, but on our homestead, it's one
of the top ways to maintain a healthy flock and to prevent diseases, parasites, and
ailments. There are a lot of other ways to get the herbs into their diet, though, rather
than just through their feed. One of the best ways to get herbs into your flock's system is through water infusions and decoctions.

What Is an Infusion?

A water infusion is much like a tea. You take your herbs (preferably dried) and steep
them in boiling water that has been removed from the stovetop. Steep for 5 to 8 minutes, then remove the herbs from the water. Voila! You have an herbal infusion. You
can offer the strained herbs to your chickens, or simply compost them.
Dosage: Use 2 to 3 teaspoons of dried herb to 8 ounces of water.

What Is a Decoction?

An herbal decoction is much like an infusion, except we use the decoction process for
more sturdy herbs, like roots, tree barks, and berries with seeds. This process involves

bringing water to a boil, adding your herb, and continuing to boil the herb for at least 10 minutes (I like to go 20 to 30 minutes). Once time is up, remove the herbs from the water, and you now have an herbal decoction! You can offer the strained herbs to your chickens, or simply compost them.

Dosage: Use 2 to 3 teaspoons of dried herb to 8 ounces of water.

Using Infusions and Decoctions in Chicken Waterers

I often use immune-boosting and antiparasitic herbs in waterers instead of in feeds. For example, I love making an infusion with thyme and garlic to place in my chick waterers on a daily basis until they reach about 8 weeks of age. This ensures they have healthy immune systems and the ability to fight off parasites, bacteria, and other nasties.

After you've made a decoction or infusion, simply add the 8 ounces of herbal preparation to your waterer. If you're filling a 1-gallon waterer, replace at least half of that with your infusion so that your chickens are receiving (at maximum) a 50 percent dilution of your infusion. This means that you'll need to create a decoction or infusion using 50 ounces of water and 12 to 18 teaspoons (or 4 to 6 tablespoons) of dried herb when creating your preparation. Discard the herbal preparation within 12 hours, as the efficacy is lessened after that time period.

We'll talk about more herbal preparations such as tinctures, salves, ointments, coop cleaners, and sprays in Chapter 10. You'll definitely return to this chapter often to reference the herbs listed and their uses.

CHAPTER

9

PREVENTING AND TREATING COMMON CHICKEN HEALTH ISSUES

We had just gotten the chickens of my dreams—French Black Copper Marans. Somehow I had convinced my husband to purchase a flock of chickens from a local chicken keeper. We made several trips, spent hundreds of dollars on chickens so that I could start my very first breeding program, and suddenly I felt like the most accomplished (but poor) person in the world.

I was still new to the entire chicken keeping thing. I was *really* new to the natural chicken keeping world, but none of that mattered in the moment. I felt like I had just scored a million dollars for the price of a quarter.

Not only was I wrong about the quality of the birds (egg color was horrible, conformation was even worse), but what I discovered a few days later was disastrous.

Every single one of these chickens that I had brought home, feeling like a million bucks, was infested with lice. *Million-dollar lice*—that's what I brought home. Suddenly I didn't feel like I was a "rich" poor person anymore.

Not only did the chickens have lice, one of the hens was already severely anemic because the lice had been feeding on her for so long. I felt horrible, and I needed a quick fix.

Back then, I didn't believe in herbal "quick fixes." So I scoured the internet in search of something that would expeditiously address the issue. I stumbled across a chicken blog that suggested poultry dust or a commercial insecticide dust to rid the chickens of the lice. I was then to follow the dusting of chemicals with 1 to 2 drops of chemical wormer, like Ivermectin or Eprinex.

I did both of those things, and I just about killed myself in the process.

After dusting all of my chickens with insecticide dust at a poultry expert's suggestion, I was covered in welts, sick as a dog, and my eyes were swollen. It worked—boy howdy, did it work. But at what expense?

From that point forward, I got serious about herbs. I was already living organically and furthering my herbal knowledge for my family. It was time to get serious about the herbal knowledge for my livestock.

In this chapter we'll touch on some of the most common chicken health issues, how to prevent them, and how to treat them naturally. I want you to keep in mind, however, that prevention is key when it comes to natural remedies. Once a chicken is unhealthy, aggressive herbal treatment must ensue, since herbs aren't a "quick fix" like chemicals are.

Recipes for some of the herbal products that I mention in this chapter can be found in Chapter 10. The corresponding page number for the herbal product is included.

I also want you to know that chicken health isn't just about herbs. Good chicken health includes a good diet, a safe and clean environment, and a decent amount of space to live in. All of these things combined will give you and your chickens the best chicken keeping experience.

Also, catching ailments and parasites early will be essential to rapidly treating your chickens naturally. Try to implement weekly or biweekly flock checks to thoroughly look over your flock and individual chickens.

Common Chicken Health Issues
Lice

As you might tell from the story above, I loathe lice with a passion. Lice are external parasites that feed on the feathers, dead skin, and blood of your chickens, causing stress, itchiness, and even anemia. If left untreated, they can even cause death. Lice tend to be found around the vents, bellies, underwings, and necks of chickens. These are some of the warmest areas on the chicken's body, and lice like to keep warm.

Prevention: Make sure your chickens have a dust bathing area available to them on a regular basis. Adding wood ash to this area will rid them of external parasites.

Treatment: Carefully dust your chickens with food-grade wood ash (preferable) or diatomaceous earth. This will kill the lice immediately. Make sure you wear a mask when doing this, or at least be careful not to breathe it in. Shake off the dust as much as possible to expel the lice from the chicken's body. This can take a while if you have a large number of chickens in your flock. For large batches of chickens, try dusting them at night, as you won't have to chase chickens around since they'll be roosting. Dust them every week, once a week, until all of the lice are gone. Otherwise, use the external parasite spray featured on page 157. Before placing the chickens back into the coop, make sure you dispose of all bedding and clean the coop with the deep-cleaning coop cleaner on page 157. Spray the roosts, nesting boxes, and all crevices to make sure you get any parasites that are hiding.

Feather Mites and Leg Mites

Mites are nasty little buggers, too. They are teeny-tiny external parasites that spread like wildfire—much more quickly than lice. Mites, much like lice, live off of dead skin cells, feathers, and the blood of your chickens. In 2018, after a very wet winter, we had our very first mite infestation *ever*. This was due to the fact that our chickens did not always have ample access to their dust bathing area, they weren't free-ranging as much because we were seeding and grading our backyard area, and we are surrounded by wild birds that can carry mites on our wooded homestead. We saw, first-hand, how herbs, diatomaceous earth, and wood ash can treat these creepy-crawly demons, and I'm happy to share our methods with you.

Prevention: Keep your coop clean and allow your chickens to dust-bathe daily. Again, just as with lice, add wood ash to your dust bathing area to help kill external parasites. Make sure your chickens have access to this area at all times, even (and especially) in the winter months. Some chicken keepers believe that adding garlic and brewer's yeast to the chickens' diet will deter mites and lice from staying on the chickens because they don't like the taste, but I've found that this isn't always true. Because mites feast not just on blood but on feathers and dead skin cells, they have other options they can chow down on. However, it doesn't hurt to add both to your chickens' regular diet.

Treatment: In a 2000 study published by the Department of Animal and Veterinary Sciences at Clemson University in South Carolina, it was found that the topical application of garlic showed great efficacy in killing mites that had infested 30 laying hens—17 New Hampshire Reds and 13 Single Comb White Leghorns. The breed of the hens had no effect on the study, therefore proving that the treatment should work on all birds. Treatment consisted of spraying the vent and abdomen of each hen with either tap water or a 10 percent garlic solution. Treatments were applied once every 7 days for 3 weeks. After the test was over, it was proven that hens that had been treated with a 10 percent garlic solution had a drastically reduced incidence of mites, with 1.8 units lower than those treated with other measures. Spraying laying hens each week for 3 weeks with a 10 percent garlic juice solution significantly decreased the incidence of mites at the 4- and 8-week mark following the start of treatment.

Begin your treatment by thoroughly cleaning out your coop and burning all of your bedding. Sweep the coop out completely, then spray down the entire coop from top to bottom with the deep-cleaning coop cleaner on page 157, concentrating intently on roosts, crevices, nesting boxes, and anywhere your chickens touch regularly. Do not add new bedding to the coop until the mites are gone. If your coop floor is slippery, add only a thin layer of bedding that can be changed daily. Use the external parasite spray featured on page 157. For leg mites, smother the mites by spraying your chickens' legs with the spray, then spread coconut oil all over their legs. Do this every few days.

Respiratory Issues

There are too many respiratory issues to name when it comes to chickens. And while I'll take the time to talk about a couple of the most common issues, I want to address respiratory illnesses as a whole. We had a couple of run-ins with these when we first started keeping chickens. Thankfully, due to preventatives and healthy breeding

Basic Chicken Maintenance

Throughout the year you'll find that you need to do some basic chicken maintenance. Here are just a few things you should consider doing on a regular basis:

- Wing clipping
- Spur removal or trimming
- Beak trimming (for those chickens that have issues)
- Yearly natural worming

genetics, we've not run into them since those early years. I attribute this to several things, which I'll talk about in the prevention portion.

Most respiratory issues begin with a bacteria, so keep that in mind when we talk about prevention and treatment. I also want to note that sometimes respiratory issues can be as simple as a dusty coop or seasonal changes, not necessarily an infection or illness. Chickens have an extremely sensitive respiratory tract. Let's not always be quick to jump on the "treat it" bandwagon. Standing back and observing the situation will help you tremendously.

A sneeze here and there, especially while foraging, is perfectly normal for a chicken. Thin, clear, runny mucus from the nose can be water that has been regurgitated, or just inflamed nasal passages from a dusty coop or a deep cleaning that you've just done. Respiratory illnesses will often present themselves in a dramatic way, such as with wheezing, coughing, gasping, and excessive sinus and eye drainage.

Prevention: Maintaining a clean and dry living environment is key to preventing bacteria from roaming into your chicken's respiratory tract. Offer echinacea, plantain, thyme, astragalus, and stinging nettle in an infusion multiple times a week—as well as in their regular feed if you're concerned about bacteria during certain times of the year—or regularly as a normal preventative. These herbs are naturally antibacterial and have antibiotic properties.

Treatment: Should a respiratory issue arise, add an herbal infusion of echinacea, plantain, thyme, astragalus, and stinging nettle to your flock's waterer multiple times a day following the infusion instructions on page 126. Quarantine your sick bird or birds so that the illness doesn't spread, and offer them the same infusion and herbs multiple times a day. You can also use the homemade respiratory tincture (see page 160) instead of the infusion. I would also add an herbal essential oil blend, which can be found through certain essential oil companies that contains laurel leaf, eucalyptus leaf, peppermint, melaleuca leaf (tea tree), lemon peel, cardamom seed, ravintsara leaf, and ravensara leaf essential oils. Apply 1 drop, diluted in 3 drops of fractionated coconut oil, to the underwings of the chicken once a day. You can also hang essential oil rags in your chicken coop for respiratory relief; see page 162 for instructions. See the other respiratory conditions below for more specific treatments.

Mycoplasma

The dreaded mycoplasma. It's the respiratory illness that chickens get and that chicken experts (or chicken keyboard ninja warriors) tell you can't be treated, *ever.* But I beg to differ, in the hope that some new studies will help eradicate this bacteria from infected flocks without the use of antibiotics. In fact, because of the cellular structure of these bacterial infections, antibiotics alone typically don't cure the chicken because the antibiotics aren't efficient enough to break down the entire bacteria, hence why chickens are often labeled "carriers for life."

Over 75 percent of the chickens in this country could be carriers (or *are* carriers) of mycoplasma. They will not show symptoms until they become stressed due to either molting, lack of protein, moving to a new coop or property, or a stressful predator attack.

Mycoplasma diseases and bacterial infections will typically present symptoms such as nasal and ocular discharge, coughing, stunted growth, and general disease symptoms (fatigue, loss of appetite, gasping, etc.). Infected chickens will also typically emit a rather foul smell from their heads. This is a telltale sign that it could be mycoplasma. Mycoplasma is mostly a respiratory issue when it comes to symptoms; however, it's much deeper than that and can cause other symptoms (that are non-respiratory) throughout the body if left untreated.

Mycoplasma isn't just transferable from chicken to chicken, but also transferable from chicken to embryo. This means that chicks that came from infected hens can be born with mycoplasma. This is why mycoplasma diseases are so scary.

In a study conducted in 2017, a breakthrough was made when studying the effects of meniran herbs (*Phyllanthus niruri L.*)—which are mostly tropical plants—with mycoplasma, specifically *Mycoplasma gallisepticum*, which causes chronic respiratory disease (CRD). When a 62.5 to 65 percent *Phyllanthus niruri L.* (gale of the wind) extract came in contact with the mycoplasma, it completely eradicated the bacteria. Because of the wealth of chemical compounds in the meniran herbs—like tannin compounds, saponins, flavonoids, and alkaloids—growth of bacteria can be inhibited and eradicated by meniran extract, according to the study.

While most of us won't have gale of the wind lying around our yard, there are some preventative measures we can take to help inhibit bacterial growth in our chickens before they become full-blown. We can also create our own meniran tinctures and extracts, if we can find the herb from a trusted source. In addition to gale of the wind, this herb also goes by the common names of stonebreaker and seed-under-leaf. It is most often found in the lower 48 states of the USA and in tropical climates.

Prevention: Many of the herbs mentioned in the feed list in the previous chapter are natural antibacterial and antiviral herbs—specifically astragalus, thyme, oregano, lemon balm, garlic, stinging nettle, and echinacea. Make sure you're providing these herbs in your chickens' feed on a regular basis, and consider adding an infusion to their waterers once or twice a week as a preventative. You can also administer the antibacterial and antiviral tincture described on page 160 as a once-a-month preventative.

Treatment: Mycoplasma is extremely aggressive. At the first sign of symptoms, immediately quarantine your sick chicken and treat the rest of the flock while treating the individual bird separately. You can make the *Phyllanthus niruri L.* tincture with a ratio of 65 percent herb and 35 percent liquid (I use 80-proof vodka). Because there is more herb than liquid, you'll need to turn the herb into a dried powder, or at least submerge the herb with a fermentation stone. You can do this by drying out your herbs in a dehydrator and then crushing them, or by purchasing pre-powdered herbs. Learn how to make a tincture on page 159. Administer the tincture (2 drops) orally, once a day, until symptoms subside, or add a dropperful of tincture to your chickens' 1-gallon waterer to treat the entire flock.

Avian Influenza (AI)

I'm taking a very brave step by adding this section to this book, but I feel that the natural chicken keeper deserves to know about the herbal preventatives and treatments for this issue. I can't make any claims that these things *will* help your flock, but they *may* help your flock, if you get my drift. I should tell you that if any time you suspect your flock has avian influenza, you should contact your local extension office to confirm this, as this is a reportable issue. AI is nothing to play around with and is extremely contagious, not just for your flock but for surrounding community flocks. It can also be carried by and spread to migratory birds.

AI, much like the flu that humans get, exhibits itself with a cough, runny nose, respiratory inflammation, and overall stress on the body. However, AI can be extremely detrimental to your flock. Once a chicken has AI, especially an aggressive strain of it, the mortality rate is between 90 and 100 percent within 48 hours. Besides that, AI spreads like wildfire, and it's highly likely that your entire flock will get it unless they have extremely healthy immune systems.

And that's where we need to begin with AI—healthy immune systems. This virus is better dealt with before your flock ever contracts it. Prevention is absolutely essential to AI, because once your flock has it, you'll need to make sure you aren't tracking it around elsewhere.

Prevention: Lemon balm and astragalus are your two big-hitting herbs when it comes to antiviral properties. These two herbs should be given to your flock regularly, either mixed in with their feed or in an infusion or decoction. Your next line of defense is echinacea, as this herb is a great immunity booster, like astragalus. You can prevent AI by giving these herbs to your flock regularly in their daily feed or their weekly infusions or decoctions. I'd also recommend adding thyme, as it supports a healthy respiratory system. You can also make the antibacterial and antiviral tincture found on page 160 and simply add a dropperful to their water a couple of times each week as a preventative.

Treatment: Your treatment options with AI have to be aggressive and quick. Nine times out of ten, herbs alone won't be aggressive or quick enough—not in the chicken world, at least. However, I want to direct you to an astragalus study published in 2013 in the *Journal of Animal Science and Biotechnology* that proved the eradication and prevention of AI within flocks with this herb. While this study was done through injection of the herb through an herbal preparation in a laboratory after pinpointing certain properties within the herb, we know that astragalus, as a whole, is an incredible immune-boosting, antiviral, and antibacterial herb. In humans, we use this herb extensively to prevent the flu and lessen the duration of the flu within our bodies by taking a daily syrup. We've seen it work, not just in our own home but through scientific studies. If a 150-pound human can take two little tablespoons of this herb once a day to prevent the flu, and multiple times a day to shorten the duration of the flu, why can't chickens take it for the very same reason if proven to work through injection in studies?

For this treatment, we would quarantine the flock members that exhibit signs of flu and treat them by offering the antibacterial and antiviral tincture found in this book—either in their waterer or orally. The instructions for prevention and treatment methods are included in the recipe.

Internal Parasites

Just as with respiratory issues, I'm going to address internal parasites as a whole. There are many different parasites that your chickens can get, but most of them are dealt with in a similar way. All chickens have some type of parasite—that's just nature at its finest. However, it's only when we see the parasites in their feces that we know there's an infestation. When we think of internal parasites, our minds automatically turn to worms. Worms are a major issue with chickens, especially those that free-range and don't have the best of immune systems. As with anything in the chicken world, a healthy immune system will ward off just about anything. Whether it's worms or other internal parasitic nasties, let's go over your prevention and treatment options.

Prevention: A healthy diet is important in the prevention of internal parasites. Stinging nettle and thyme are two of the best antiparasitic herbs you can add to your chickens' diet on a regular basis. You may also notice that they are two of my favorite herbs to place in an infusion for your chicken waterers. However, simply adding them to your chickens' feed helps tremendously. I also recommend allowing your chickens to pasture-range on rotation as much as possible. This dramatically cuts down on the possibility of internal parasites. You can also offer the internal parasite tincture on page 158 once or twice a month as a natural preventative, as it includes other herbs, like black walnut hulls and garlic, that are aggressive antiparasitics when extracted in a tincture.

The Truth about Pumpkinseeds

While it is popular to suggest pumpkin and pumpkinseeds as a natural antiparasitic, it is actually the extraction of the medicinal properties in the pumpkinseeds that is an antiparasitic. You can continue to give your chickens pumpkin and pumpkinseeds, but you probably won't get rid of a worm infestation with them. Your best bet is to make a tincture out of the seeds to keep on hand when you need it, or add pumpkinseeds to the internal parasite tincture recipe on page 158.

Treatment: When you've discovered that you have an internal parasite issue, you'll want to begin treating immediately. Use the internal parasite tincture twice a week for four weeks. If you see that the parasites have been eradicated after four weeks, simply begin giving your chickens regular antiparasitic herbs in their diet. If not all of the parasites are eradicated, drop down to once a week for two more weeks and then reevaluate.

Internal Bacterial Issues

Bacterial issues such as coccidiosis and enteritis are very common in backyard flocks, especially in living conditions that are wet or not rotated. Chicken keepers in the Pacific Northwest can find themselves with internal bacterial issues often, due to the rainy and warm weather conditions. As with other chicken health issues, most bacterial ailments are treated in a similar way. Let's go over prevention and treatment options.

Prevention: Keeping the living conditions of your flock as clean and dry as possible will be your biggest challenge. If your flock is rotating on pasture or free-ranging, this will be easier. But if you have a confined flock, try adding outdoor bedding, like wood chips or mulch, to your chicken run area to help water dissipate more easily. Your next step is, once again, adding herbs to their diet. Antibacterial herbs and infusions, like astragalus, echinacea, garlic, lemon balm, oregano, stinging nettle, and thyme, are perfect additions to your flock's weekly or daily diet. Feeding antibacterial herbs such as nasturtium and purple dead nettle, either freely while ranging or by the handful, will also help keep down the bacteria in their digestive tracts. Offer the antibacterial and antiviral tincture on page 160 once or twice a month as a preventative.

Treatment: Typical bacterial infection symptoms are lethargy, listlessness, drooping wings, discolored feces (diarrhea), and pale combs and wattles. Immediate treatment is key. Offer the antibacterial and antiviral tincture once a day until symptoms subside.

Sour Crop and Crop Impaction

It sounds like a bad case of fungus in the cornfield, but no, we're definitely talking about chickens! The "crop" of the chicken can be found at the base of the throat. It's often weird to feel little bits of food inside the crop with your hand. Crop impaction happens when a foreign object or a nervous system issue doesn't allow digestion to occur naturally from the crop to the proventriculus (the "stomach"). Symptoms include loss of appetite, listlessness, and a hard, firm crop. Sour crop is a yeast infection in the crop, causing the crop wall to thicken. This happens when the bacterial balance of the chicken becomes imbalanced, therefore causing bad bacteria, like *Candida*, to grow and cause digestive issues.

While sour crop is a bacterial issue, it can be caused by an impacted crop. Ultimately, both issues occur when the crop cannot fully empty itself. You'll need to figure out whether it's sour crop or an impacted crop. You can do this by checking on your chicken first thing in the morning. Before eating, if the chicken's crop is still full and hard, it means that the crop is impacted. If the crop is full and fluid-filled, it means your chicken more than likely has sour crop.

Prevention: Try not to offer your chickens large pieces of feed or foraged items. Certainly, with pasture-ranging we can't be with our chickens all day long, but we can absolutely control the treats and table scraps we give them (like too much bread or hard items). Your next course of prevention is to offer an ample supply of fresh water with raw organic apple cider vinegar (ACV) on a regular basis. This will help keep the bacteria in the crop balanced. Offering your chickens antibacterial herbs will also help.

Treatment: You'll want to remove the chicken from the rest of your flock and withhold food from her for the first 24 to 48 hours. Offer only grit, clean water, and your waterer with ACV and herbs to help prevent further infection. If the crop is impacted, gently massage it after the chicken has eaten a bit of grit. Some experts suggest gently turning the chicken upside down while massaging, in an attempt to remove the impaction from the crop, but this is a risky move, as the chicken can inhale the crop contents or liquid. You can try adding just a bit of olive oil to the crop via an eyedropper and massaging, but you take the chance of it going rancid if it doesn't eliminate itself from the crop. Impacted crop is extremely dangerous for your chicken, and in some cases may require a trip to the vet or a cull. Continue to offer liquids with your antibacterial herbs and ACV for sour crop multiple times a day until symptoms subside. You can administer the antibacterial and antiviral tincture found on page 160 once a day until symptoms subside.

Bumblefoot

I've dealt with bumblefoot twice in my life—once with someone else's chicken, and once with my own—but in two different ways. Bumblefoot normally occurs when a chicken gets something stuck in its foot. It can be a splinter, a piece of glass, or a thorn. Whatever the case may be, chickens don't have opposable thumbs and tweezers; therefore, if the issue doesn't resolve itself, it will cause an infection in the foot. It can also come from an improper roost, causing friction on the foot and allowing bacteria to get into it. Sometimes bumblefoot can happen from a simple cut as well. Once it occurs, we now have a staph infection to deal with. If caught early enough, the issue can be resolved easily with a salve or with essential oils. But if left to go on too long, the infection will need to be surgically extracted, which can easily be done at home. If not treated, bumblefoot can spread up the leg and ultimately result in death.

A Funny Bumble

I've performed a surgical removal of infection once, and it ended badly for me, not for the chicken. After opening the foot, I was having trouble squeezing the infection out (think of it as a giant pimple). I kept squeezing and squeezing until finally it shot out like a cannon . . . right into my mouth! The chicken went flying into the air, I went running, but thankfully all of the infection had come out. My goodness, what a horrible experience it was! Don't do this—don't be me!

The symptoms of bumblefoot begin with a red or swollen foot or area of the foot-pad. Once the issue has progressed to a full-blown infection, a dark scab may form on the bottom of the foot, and prominent swelling will occur between the toes.

Prevention: Make sure there aren't any obvious obstacles for your chickens when they roam. Splinters on pallets are a major issue; jumping down off a roost that is too high can also be an issue. Be aware of the issues that could arise when it comes to your chickens' safety in the barnyard.

Treatment: As I mentioned earlier, there are two different herbal treatments for this. The first one is very simple and noninvasive; the second one, well, you're going to be all up in your chicken's personal bubble. If you catch the infection before it becomes a full-blown bumble, your quickest route to healing will be essential oils. Add 1 drop each of tea tree, oregano, and lavender to a small bowl with 6 drops of fractionated coconut oil. Rub the infected area with the oil liberally, then wrap the foot with medical wrap and allow the chicken to go about her day. Replace the dressing every evening as she goes to roost so that the oils can seep into her foot all night long. You can re-dress midday if you'd like, but that will be up to you and how aggressive the infection is. Note: If there is a scab present, you may only have to remove the scab and squeeze the infection out and then dress.

TIP

Don't want to use essential oils? Try using black drawing salve instead; recipe on page 155.

Your next level of treatment is surgery. Sterilize a very sharp knife or scalpel with vodka or alcohol, and make a small incision in the shape of an X on the foot where the infection is. Apply pressure and squeeze out all of the infection. Flush the hole with a solution of 1 tablespoon of raw honey and 1 to 2 tablespoons of water; the raw honey is a natural antibacterial. Mix 1 drop each of tea tree, oregano, and lavender into a small bowl with 6 drops of fractionated coconut oil. Apply to the foot to cleanse and disinfect the area. Wrap the foot and allow to heal, applying the essential oils once a day until the hole is completely closed.

Egg Binding

Egg binding is more common than most chicken keepers may realize. This happens when an egg becomes stuck in the hen's vent, not allowing subsequent eggs to be released. An egg-bound hen will become lethargic, have a droopy tail, will walk differently, may lay and rest frequently, and may often try to lay the egg, but without success. This is an extremely tricky situation to navigate, but it can be done. Egg binding happens when a young hen tries to pass an egg that is too large, an egg in a regular hen isn't in the proper position to be laid, a hen is lacking calcium in her diet, or there is a bacterial issue. Whatever the cause, that egg has to come out.

Prevention: Make sure your chickens are getting enough calcium and antibacterial and immune-boosting herbs in their diet. Your hens should also always have a clean and quiet place to lay their eggs.

Treatment: Treatments are different for each egg-bound hen and chicken keeper, but here are your main options. You may have to try just one, or you may have to try them all before the egg releases. Whatever options you try, be sure to offer your hen astragalus, basil, and chamomile in a water infusion to help keep her relaxed and reduce stress on her body during this time. Note: Keep your egg-bound hen in a dark and quiet place, separate from the flock, while treating her.

Option 1: Lubricate your fingers with a natural and organic (if possible) lubricant jelly or the antibacterial ointment found on page 154. It's best to do this with thin latex gloves so that your fingernails don't scratch the delicate lining of your hen's vent. Gently maneuver your fingers into the vent to see if you can feel the egg. If you can, you know for sure that the hen is egg-bound. You can lubricate the vent and egg to see if it will loosen enough to come out on its own the next time the hen goes to lay her egg. You may have to do this a couple of times in one day for it to release. If this method is unsuccessful after a few hours, move on to your next option.

Option 2: Place the hen in a warm bath, just enough to cover her vent and abdomen. The warm water will allow the muscles in her body to relax, therefore increasing the likelihood she'll release the egg. You may need to do this several times through-out the day, along with lubrication, to help relax the muscles and release the egg. But if this still doesn't work, you may have to go with the last option, which can be extremely dangerous.

Option 3: Try options 1 and 2 for at least 24 to 48 hours before trying option 3, as option 3 can be extremely risky. However, your chicken could potentially die whether you try this option or not if the egg doesn't release. This is a last-resort option. Note: Work slowly and gently at all times.

With gloves and a lubricant (or antibacterial ointment), try to extract the white and yolk of the egg by using a thick needle syringe to poke a hole into the end of the egg. After the contents of the egg have been taken out, try cracking the egg, keeping as much of the shell as intact as possible. Once all of the egg has been removed, flush the vent area out with a raw honey and water solution to clean it thoroughly, being careful not to flush any shell or egg contents farther up into the vent.

Offer your hen antibacterial herbs for the next few days, and flush her vent out fre-quently with a warm chamomile, raw honey, and water solution to prevent bacterial infection and to soothe the vent.

General Cuts and Open Wounds

One morning, our sweet Barred Rock, Elizabeth (my grandmother's middle name), was attacked by a predator. We aren't sure what, exactly, it was, but from the signs I assume it was a bear or fox. The gash on her back was extensive, right down to bone. It was the dead of summer and fly strike had already set in. This happens when flies lay eggs on the wounds or open flesh of an animal. I needed something that would work quickly. As you know, a chicken's skin is very thin, so stitches at this point weren't really an option. We were able to completely heal her within a few days by

Raw Honey to the Rescue!

When in a pinch, if you don't have any herbs or essential oils on hand, you can use raw or manuka honey, which is thought to be up to four times more powerful in antibacterial properties than regular raw honey, for just about anything. It is a natural antibacterial and helps cleanse and heal wounds and other illnesses. If nothing else, keep raw or manuka honey on hand! It can be added to waterers, infusions and decoctions, salves and ointments, and more.

using essential oils and herbal ointment. The essential oils also killed the fly eggs that had already been laid. You can use these same methods for general cuts or for much larger open wounds.

Prevention: The most obvious prevention is to make sure your chickens' environment is chicken friendly with no safety hazards, including ways for predators to get to them.

Treatment: Clean the wound thoroughly with warm water. Mix 1 drop each of tea tree, lavender, chamomile, and oregano essential oils with 8 to 10 drops of fractionated coconut oil. This will not only help soothe and heal but also cleanse the wound. Smear a bit of the oil mixture on the wound, coating it entirely, and the surrounding area. Dress as needed, or leave to air dry. After 12 hours, reapply the oils or use the antibacterial ointment on page 154. Reapply either the oils or ointment twice a day until the wound closes.

My Chicken's Herbal Medicine Cabinet

While there are a lot of products you can have handy, here's what I tend to keep on hand at all times:

Medical Supplies

- Thin latex gloves
- Small, sharp knife or scalpel
- Self-adhesive medical wraps
- Rubbing alcohol
- Syringes
- Eyedropper
- Spray bottles
- General first-aid tools

Herbal Products

- Antibacterial ointment (recipe on page 154)
- Black drawing salve (recipe on page 155)
- Antibacterial and antiviral tincture (recipe on page 160)
- Raw honey
- Manuka honey
- Essential oils
- External parasite spray (recipe on page 157)
- Dried herbs

When you take on chicken keeping, you take on becoming a chicken vet of sorts as well. While I've covered just a small sampling of chicken issues, learning these basics will help you when your chickens need your care. It's been rare for our chickens to get sick or hurt, so that's why there isn't a more extensive section on diseases or chicken health issues in this book.

Learning about common chicken issues and how to treat and prevent them naturally will help you have the confidence you need when a problem arises. It will also encourage you to keep natural remedies and medical supplies on hand at all times.

CHAPTER

10

HERBAL TREATS AND MEDICINAL PRODUCTS FOR CHICKENS

There's something about harvesting herbs in the early morning that really brightens the soul. Living the farm life has taught me how to slow down and enjoy the simplicity of dirt and plants. We try to be as sustainable as possible in our practices by leaving behind enough herbs that will continue to provide for us for years to come (whether it's wild foraging or growing our own).

As an herbalist, extending my knowledge of herbs into chicken keeping seemed only natural and complementary. It's still hard to find good, honest, chemical-free herbal remedies and products for the homestead. So, I decided to make my own.

In this chapter you'll find all of my favorite herbal products for chickens. While there are some we don't use often, I still try to make them at least once a year to keep on hand for my herbal remedies and products cabinet. I've also included herbal treats for chickens. They are incredibly simple and easy to make, and you may find that you'll start tweaking them for your own natural chicken keeping needs.

Important: Herbal oint-
ments and salves should
be tossed out after their
one-year shelf life. Dried
herbs, in general, should
be restocked after 12 to 18
months. You should always
use dried herbs
when creating
your herbal
products.

I often chuckle when I see name-brand
"chicken remedies" touted by bloggers and well-
known chicken enthusiasts. On our homestead,
we make our own brand, and I wouldn't have
it any other way, and neither should you—talk
about sustainable living!

Use these herbal remedies for the ailments
mentioned throughout this book, or make
them to have on hand for when you need them.

HERBAL OATMEAL

One of my favorite ways to get herbs into all of my chickens—especially routine maintenance herbs—is to use homemade oatmeal. Whip up a batch of this once or twice a month to help get some amazing herbs and a boost of minerals into your chickens, but don't offer your chickens oatmeal more than once a week. Some herbs to consider for this are thyme, oregano, astragalus, calendula, chamomile, comfrey, echinacea, nasturtium, and garlic.

5 cups water
4 cups steel-cut oatmeal
1 large handful each flaxseeds, chia seeds, and herbs of choice
4–5 tablespoons blackstrap molasses

Method:

1. Bring water to a boil on stovetop, and add oatmeal.

2. Cook for 5 minutes on medium heat until water is absorbed.

3. Remove from heat and place oatmeal into a large bowl. Add remaining ingredients and mix well.

4. Allow to cool to room temperature before offering to your chickens.

5. Give once a week or every few weeks for herbal maintenance!

HERBAL TREAT BLOCK

In the wintertime when the grass isn't growing here on the East Coast and my chickens need something to look forward to, I really enjoy making herbal treat blocks for them. We offer birdseed to our native birds throughout this time of year, so why not our chickens? They get some extra love with herbs and more.

2 cups scratch grains (or your homemade chicken feed)
1 cup wheat germ
1/2 cup raisins or Craisins
1/2 cup black oil sunflower seeds
1/2 cup oyster shell
2 tablespoons thyme, dried
2 tablespoons echinacea leaves, crushed
2 tablespoons stinging nettle, dried and crushed
4 eggs, plus their crushed eggshells
1 cup molasses
1/2 cup coconut oil or lard

Method:

1. Preheat oven to 400°F.

2. In a large bowl, combine all the dry ingredients well.

3. In a separate bowl, combine all the wet ingredients well.

4. Add the wet ingredients to the dry ingredients and mix well.

5. Spread the mixture in a greased pan about 2 inches thick. You can make a large batch on a cookie sheet and break it into pieces once done, or get creative and bake the mixture in mini block shapes or cake pans for a more individual serving approach.

6. Bake for 20 minutes or until golden and firm.

7. Remove from the oven and allow to sit for 10 minutes. Transfer to a cooling rack.

8. Offer this herbal boredom-buster to your chickens as needed!

The Big Molt

Your adult hens will go through a molt every year, normally around late summer or fall. This is the process of losing their old feathers and growing new ones. They will need extra protein to help them during this time, and extra immune-boosting herbs. Offer the herbal treat block to your molting girls each season!

ANTIBACTERIAL OINTMENT

The herbs in this ointment all have antibacterial properties and are incredible at healing the body naturally. Use this salve just as you would any over-the-counter antibiotic ointment or salve. It works fabulously on wounds, cuts, and other general chicken health issues.

3 ounces calendula-infused oil
0.5 ounce beeswax
10 drops tea tree essential oil
10 drops oregano essential oil

10 drops vitamin E oil

1 tablespoon manuka honey

Method:

1. In a double boiler, melt together the calendula-infused oil and beeswax.

2. Turn the heat off and add the essential oils, vitamin E oil, and manuka honey.

3. Quickly pour your salve into tins or a jar. Allow to cool completely, then cap, label, and store for up to one year. You can whip the ointment with a whisk or immersion blender if you'd like, but it's not a hard salve so it works well either way.

BLACK DRAWING SALVE

If there's one salve you should keep on hand at all times, it's this one. It is so versatile when it comes to ailments. Use it on frostbitten rooster combs, bumblefoot, wounds, irritations—the possibilities are endless. This salve not only soothes and heals, but also draws out infection and helps with inflammation. Note: Activated charcoal and bentonite clay can be purchased from most health food stores and online. They can sometimes be found in the health and beauty section of regular stores as well.

6 tablespoons calendula-infused oil

3 tablespoons plantain-infused oil

1 tablespoon coconut oil (or sweet almond, castor, or grape seed oil)

1 tablespoon beeswax

1 tablespoon activated charcoal

1 tablespoon bentonite clay

10 drops tea tree essential oil

10 drops lavender essential oil (optional)

Storage tins or jars

Method:

1. Add about 1 inch of water to a saucepan and turn on to medium heat. You're making a double boiler so that your oils won't be touching direct heat.

2. In a glass or tin jar, add calendula oil, plantain oil, coconut oil, and beeswax. Place the jar in the saucepan to create a double boiler. Stir oils and beeswax until melted completely.

3. Add charcoal and clay, and mix well. If you need a thicker consistency, add a little more clay.

4. Remove the jar from heat, and add essential oils. I like to add tea tree and

lavender because of their healing properties, but the possibilities are endless.

5. Optional: If you'd like a more whipped consistency, leave the salve in the jar until almost hardened, then whip it with a whisk or immersion blender.

6. Pour the salve into a new jar or individual tins—something that you can easily dip the salve out of. Allow to cool completely, then cap tightly, label, and store for up to a year in your medicine cabinet.

7. When needed, use a small amount topically. Cover with a bandage for up to 12 hours before rinsing off.

MAINTENANCE COOP CLEANER

There are a lot of complicated ways to make a coop cleaner, but when you're a busy homesteader, a maintenance coop cleaner is really all you need. This is where I utilize essential oils the most. They are quick and easy to grab off my shelf instead of waiting 4 weeks for herbs to infuse. Try these essential oils in your coop cleaner, and mix and match them as you see fit. The basis of this cleaner is to help repel bugs, flies, and other pests and to make your coop smell lovely. Spray down your roosts, walls, and nesting boxes (not the bedding) with this cleaner once a day for a lovely air freshening! Or use it weekly as a natural cleaner.

Non-chlorinated water
Witch hazel
6 drops tea tree essential oil
6 drops lemongrass essential oil
8 drops oregano essential oil
2 drops clove essential oil
3 drops sage essential oil

Method:

1. Fill a 16-ounce spray bottle a little less than

three-quarters of the way with water. Then add 1 part witch hazel, leaving room to add the essential oils.

2. Add the essential oils to the bottle, and shake well to combine. Shake before each use. Store in a temperature-controlled area for up to 6 months.

DEEP-CLEANING COOP CLEANER

While maintenance coop cleaners are amazing, sometimes for an external parasite issue or when an extra-strength cleaner is needed, this deep-cleaning coop cleaner is the spray I make up and grab off the shelf!

20 cloves garlic, peeled and smashed (or 1 ounce garlic extract)
45 drops eucalyptus essential oil
30 drops lavender essential oil
30 drops peppermint essential oil
20 drops cinnamon bark essential oil
20 drops melissa (lemon balm) essential oil
15 drops tea tree essential oil
2 tablespoons white vinegar (unless using garlic extract)
Water

Method:

1. In a 16-ounce glass spray bottle, combine the garlic (or extract) and essential oils. If using smashed garlic, allow it to sit for several hours before using the spray (overnight is even better).

2. If using garlic extract, do not add white vinegar. Simply fill the rest of the bottle up with water three-quarters of the way full. However, if using smashed garlic, add vinegar at this point.

3. Shake the bottle well before each spray. Store in a temperature-controlled area, like a pantry or medicine cabinet. Dispose of after 6 months.

EXTERNAL PARASITE SPRAY

This external parasite spray is almost identical to the deep-cleaning coop spray, but a little different. Follow the directions closely on how to use the spray. Make sure you spray down your coop each time you treat your chickens.

20 cloves garlic, peeled and smashed (or 1 ounce garlic extract)
45 drops eucalyptus essential oil

30 drops lavender essential oil
30 drops peppermint essential oil
20 drops cinnamon bark essential oil
20 drops melissa (lemon balm) essential oil
2 tablespoons white vinegar (unless using garlic extract)
Water

Method:

1. In a 16-ounce glass spray bottle, combine the garlic (or extract) and essential oils. If using smashed garlic, allow it to sit for several hours before using the spray (overnight is even better).

2. If using garlic extract, do not add white vinegar. Simply fill the rest of the bottle up with water three-quarters of the way full. However, if using smashed garlic, add vinegar at this point.

3. Shake the bottle well before each spray.

4. Spray directly on the skin of the chicken, concentrating only on the neck, the vent area, and the top of the tail where the oil gland is. I also spray their feet and the base of the roosting bar so that when they lay back down on their feet and roost, the mixture gets onto their bellies. Note: Do this treatment at night after they've gone to roost to ensure the spray stays on for an extended period of time.

5. Continue this treatment daily for 2 weeks, then twice a week for 2 additional weeks, to rid your chickens of mites.

INTERNAL PARASITE TINCTURE

When worms and other internal parasites arise, you'll want to have this tincture premade. I make this once a year just in case I need it. You can also use it as a monthly preventative. Note: If you'd like to add pumpkinseed to this tincture, add 1 ounce of pumpkinseed and 1 extra ounce of vodka.

0.5 ounce clove, ground
0.5 ounce black walnut hulls, ground (or powdered)
1 ounce thyme, dried
1 ounce stinging nettle, dried
1 ounce grapefruit seed (optional)
2 garlic cloves, smashed
16 ounces 80-proof vodka

Method:

1. Premeasure all herbs and vodka. If omitting the grapefruit seed, reduce vodka by 1 ounce.

2. Place all the herbs in a large glass jar. Cover the herbs with the vodka, making sure they are submerged. If it helps, you can crush the herbs a bit before doing this step.

3. Shake your tincture liberally and then set it in a cool pantry or cupboard, away from extreme temperature changes and direct sunlight. Shake your tincture every day (multiple times, if you want) for 4 to 6 weeks.

4. After 4 to 6 weeks, strain your tincture from the jar. Pour your strained tincture into a colored glass eye-dropper bottle, label, and store in a cool place until ready to use.

5. Use 1 dropperful in chicken waterer or administer 2 drops by mouth.

6. Use tincture as a preventative once a month by mouth or in chicken waterer, according to your own schedule. If parasites arise, use once every 4 to 8 hours for 2 to 3 weeks.

HOW TO MAKE YOUR OWN TINCTURE

You can create your own tincture by following these simple steps. Utilize the herbs described in Chapter 8 to make your own tinctures for your chickens! Tinctures should be created using either a 1:2 or 1:4 ratio. A 1:4 ratio is the highest it should be for chicken tinctures (1 ounce herbs to 4 ounces vodka). If you don't wish to use alcohol, you can use glycerine.

1 ounce dried herb(s)
4 ounces 80-proof (or higher) vodka

1. Add the premeasured herb(s) and vodka to a glass jar.

2. Cap tightly, shake well, and set in the pantry for 4 weeks. Shake daily.

3. After 4 weeks, strain the herb(s) from the tincture and bottle the liquid in a colored glass eye-dropper bottle. Store at room temperature in your medicine cabinet or pantry for up to 2 years.

Note: If you use multiple types of herbs, just make sure your ratio goes up. For example, if you're doing 2 ounces of herbs, you'll need to use 8 ounces of vodka, and so on.

ANTIBACTERIAL AND ANTIVIRAL TINCTURE

Among the most common ailments for chickens are bacterial and viral issues. I like to use this tincture in my waterers during bird migrations, when avian flu and other respiratory issues are more prevalent. It's also a necessary tincture for internal bacterial issues.

1 ounce echinacea (root or leaves), dried
0.5 ounce wormwood, dried
0.5 ounce thyme, dried
0.5 ounce chicory, dried
2 garlic cloves, smashed
10 ounces 80-proof vodka

Method:

1. Add all the herbs to a glass jar and cover with vodka.

2. Cap tightly and set in a dark, temperature-controlled space (like a pantry or cupboard) for 4 weeks. Shake daily.

3. After 4 weeks, strain the tincture into a colored glass eye-dropper bottle. Label and store in a medicine cabinet or cupboard. Administer by placing 1 dropperful into a gallon waterer, or administer 2 drops orally. Administer twice a day until symptoms subside.

RESPIRATORY TINCTURE

We always automatically think "disaster" when a chicken sneezes, but that's just not always the case. Making this respiratory tincture ahead of time will help keep your chooks healthy and heal them quickly when you actually do need it.

0.5 ounce echinacea, dried
0.75 ounce astragalus, dried
0.25 ounce plantain, dried
0.5 ounce thyme, dried
0.5 ounce stinging nettle, dried
10 ounces 80-proof (or higher) vodka

Method:

1. Add all the herbs to a glass jar and cover with vodka.

2. Cap tightly and set in a dark, temperature-controlled space (like a pantry or cupboard) for 4 weeks. Shake daily.

3. After 4 weeks, strain the tincture into a colored glass eye-dropper bottle. Label and store in a medicine cabinet or cupboard. Administer by placing 1 dropperful into a gallon waterer, or administer 2 drops orally. Administer twice a day until symptoms subside.

ESSENTIAL OIL BLENDS

Herbs are getting more attention in the chicken world than they used to, but essential oils are still a bit of a taboo subject. The interesting thing, however, is that essential oils are tested more often in poultry studies than actual herbs. I think that, in and of itself, this has a lot to say about the efficacy of essential oils on poultry. Let's go over a few blends that can help your flock when you need them most. Note: When using essential oils on your flock, only use 1 drop (or less) of oil blend per bird. Always dilute straight essential oils before treating your flock.

Respiratory Blend

2 drops each peppermint, eucalyptus, tea tree, lemon, and cardamom oils
20 drops fractionated coconut oil

Apply 1 drop of this blend under the wings or on an essential oil rag (instructions to follow) when your chickens need some respiratory aid.

Cuts and Wounds Blend

2 drops each tea tree (melaleuca), oregano, lavender, and chamomile oils
16 drops fractionated coconut oil

Use 1 drop of this blend on your chicken's wound as necessary.

Calming Blend

2 drops each chamomile, marjoram, and lavender oils
20 drops fractionated coconut oil

This blend works best on an essential oil rag during times of stress, after predator attacks, or in the winter months.

Pest Control Blend

2 drops each tea tree (melaleuca), peppermint, and eucalyptus oils
12 drops fractionated coconut oil

Apply 1 drop directly on the skin of the bird, or place on an essential oil rag.

ESSENTIAL OIL RAGS

I often use these rags when I need to aromatically soothe or help keep pests away from my livestock. You simply sprinkle drops of essential oils or oil blends on rag strips and hang them strategically around the barnyard. Keep in mind that these rags are used in open rather than confined spaces. If you're using them in extra-small hutches or coops, cut each recipe in half. Use this recipe as a basis for all your rag recipes.

5 strips of old rags
10 to 20 drops of essential oils (total)

Add the essential oils to the rag strips (10 to 20 drops total, not per rag). These 5 strips will fill an 8-by-8-foot coop with their aroma. If you have a larger space, you'll need to make more rag strips and space them strategically throughout the building.

We're not in the business of having sick chickens on our homestead. I'm a firm believer that offering your chickens a natural diet and preventative herbs will help them be the happiest and healthiest they can be. But I am also well aware that sometimes things happen, and we need to keep herbal remedies on hand. I hope that this chapter broadened your horizons and allowed you to gain some herbal knowledge in the do-it-yourself health field of chicken keeping!

Glorious Egg Layers

SUMMER MORNINGS ON OUR LITTLE HOMESTEAD are my favorite. The dew sits on the blades of grass, the wind blows through the trees, and in the distance there's a chicken singing her egg song at the top of her lungs. She's like that old lady at church who stands behind you, blaring her sweet praises to Jesus, but can't carry a tune to save her soul . . . bless her heart.

That song (from the chicken, not the old lady) is a daily reminder that I have fresh eggs ready and waiting for me in the coop when I go to collect them. And my goodness, it is a glorious song indeed, no matter how loud it may be.

This next part is devoted to the glorious egg layers in the natural chicken keeper's life. They deserve a section all of their own, because when the spring sun starts shinin', those ladies start singin', and that means there's going to be fresh eggs in the frying pan, friends.

THE INCREDIBLE EGG
AND EGG LAYER

I highly despised eggs growing up. In fact, I think I despised them so much that I've already mentioned this at the beginning of the book. You could get me to eat eggs, but only if they were smothered in ketchup. Isn't that the way parents always get their kids to eat things that they don't like?

Even into early adulthood, eggs just weren't my thing, man. I turned my nose up at those "butt nuggets" like they were exactly that—butt nuggets. Now it's just a cute term I like to call farm-fresh chicken eggs. C'mon, you know you're chuckling. And I really love my chickens' eggs.

There's truly a difference between factory eggs and home-raised eggs, especially from chickens that are on pasture. Pasture-raised chicken yolks are a deep, rich orange color, while factory store-bought eggs are pale and yellow. The difference in color occurs when free-range chickens eat more beta-carotene, grass, protein, bugs, and vitamins. They do this from natural foraging and natural additives in their diet. Omega-3s are abundant in pasture-raised chickens' eggs as well.

Homegrown vs. Store-Bought Eggs

Homegrown eggs have:

- **more vitamins**
- **more omega-3 fatty acids (good for brain health!)**
- **more beta-carotene**
- **less cholesterol**
- **less saturated fat**

Besides the obvious health benefits, homegrown eggs are easier to store, have a longer shelf life, and don't require washing. They come in various sizes and colors, and they are a joy to collect each day!

How to Store and Preserve Your Eggs

Chicken eggs are extremely easy to store and preserve. You can simply collect your eggs and store them at room temperature on the counter, in the refrigerator, or in a root cellar. Storing in the refrigerator or a cool root cellar will prolong the shelf life of the eggs (up to 4 or more weeks). Otherwise, eggs can be stored at room temperature safely for about 2 weeks and then moved to a cool or refrigerated area for several more weeks before discarding.

Whichever way you decide to store your eggs, *remember not to wash them*. Washing them removes the protective bloom from the outside of the egg. Not only that, but washing them can cause bacteria and other bad things to leach through the eggshell (like salmonella), crippling the freshness and safety of your farm-fresh egg.

If you have an abundance of eggs, however, it may be overload for the counter, the fridge, *and* the root cellar! Here are some ways that you can preserve your eggs so that you have fresh eggs on hand in the winter months and all year long:

Freeze your eggs. This is the most common way to preserve eggs. Simply crack your

eggs open into a bowl, whisk together, and place the eggs into silicone ice cube trays. Freeze until solid, then pop them out and put them into a freezer bag for storage.

Water-glass your eggs. The technique known as "water glassing" has been used since the 1800s. The ingredient called "water glass" is liquid sodium silicate, which is a preservative. You should only use fresh, clean eggs without any dirt, mud, or debris. Refer to the National Center for Home Food Preservation website for more information, https://nchfp.uga.edu/.

Here's an excerpt taken from *The Boston Cooking-School Cook Book* by Fannie Farmer, written in 1896, that explains the technique:

> *Only use fresh eggs which have been wiped clean, but not washed. Mix eleven parts water with one part water glass in an earthenware crock. Place eggs in solution leaving about two inches of liquid above the eggs. One quart of water glass will treat about 16 dozen eggs.*

OR

Mix one part water glass with ten parts cooled, boiled water and pour into a large, stone crock. Wipe off fresh eggs with a flannel cloth and place in solution (eggs should be covered with 2). Cover crock and store in a cool, dry place.

Important: Water glass should be handled with care and kept out of the reach of children!

Freeze-dry your eggs. This method is probably one of the best methods to use, as your eggs will be preserved for at least 10 years. Your eggs can be stored in Mylar bags or air-sealed containers until ready to be rehydrated. Follow the manufacturer's instructions for your freeze dryer.

Why Should I Preserve My Eggs?

We're talking about egg preservation, but why is it so important? *Don't chickens lay eggs every day?* The truth is, chickens only lay through the sunniest parts of the year—late winter through autumn. About three months out of the year (sometimes more), their egg production decreases or becomes nonexistent. Preserving your eggs at peak season will come in handy when you need them!

There are other time-tested egg preservation methods, but these are the most natural ways to preserve your eggs so that they remain safe and natural for your family. But the best part about fresh eggs is eating them while they are fresh!

The Life of the Egg Layer

She wakes up in the morning, jumps into the nesting box, and settles down to start her job—laying her daily egg. Out pops the prize, she sings her beautiful egg song, and off about her regular day she goes. Throughout the day she'll feast on grass, bugs, rodents, wild edibles, grit, and more. She'll drink water like it's going out of style.

Later in the day she might decide to take a dust bath, clean and oil her feathers (with the oil gland at the base of her tail feathers), and just hang out with the rest of her girls.

The life of an egg layer, what a beautiful life it is!

The Egg Cycle

It takes a hen about 24 to 26 hours to create one egg in her reproductive system. The egg is made up of several different parts—the shell, the egg white (albumin), the chalazae (the little white connective strings inside), and the yolk. The egg starts as just the yolk from the hen's reproductive system. The yolk grows during the ovulation period, then releases and is surrounded by the chalazae, which helps keep the egg yolk suspended in the middle of the egg.

TIP

Egg production drops off after 18 months of age. However, we've had chickens lay several times a week up until the age of 7.

The hen's egg will move through the oviduct and be surrounded by the albumin and, finally, the eggshell. The eggshell is what takes the longest in the egg cycle. It can take about 20 hours for the calcium and minerals to be deposited around the egg. In fact, the longer the egg stays in the oviduct, the more colorful it will become if you have a colorful-egg-laying breed. For example, if you have a blue egg layer, the longer that egg stays inside, the bluer it will become.

So the next time you collect those eggs, remember just how much work went into it!

Pampering Your Egg Layers

While I'm not a huge advocate for all the bells and whistles that many people give their hens on a regular basis, I do enjoy a bit of pampering when I've put in a hard day's work myself, so I'm sure my hens do as well.

Here are some ways you can make sure your hens are comfortable and not stressed during their egg-laying years:

- Add curtains to your nesting boxes, or make sure the nesting boxes are very private. This makes your hen feel safe and comfortable, and more willing to lay in the box!

- Offer adaptogen (stress-relieving) herbs like astragalus, holy basil, and rosemary to her diet and nesting box.

- Spruce up the nesting boxes every morning when you let your hens out. A clean nesting box is a comfortable nesting box!

- Make sure there's plenty of sunlight coming into the coop during the day so that she can see her way to the nesting area.

- Offer homemade herbal treats to spoil your hens (see recipe on page 153).

Your hens will thank you after a hard day's work, and you'll thank them when you taste those delicious eggs they've offered you!

5

The Chicken Business

THE FIRST TIME SOMEONE HANDED ME a five-dollar bill for a dozen eggs was an ah-ha moment. I was only charging $3 per dozen, but the customer told me, "Your eggs are the best eggs I can find. They are worth five dollars, so own it!"

From that point forward, I started charging $5 per dozen for my non-GMO, free-range eggs. And every single egg customer bought them without question.

As a chicken keeper who raises his or her flock as naturally as possible, you're going to have people who are ready and willing to partake of your bounty. Maybe they are living in the city and can't grow their own. Or maybe they are on their way to growing their own but still need your help. Whatever it may be, you've found a way to make extra money from your everyday lifestyle. Let's walk through how to have a success in each venture.

CHAPTER

12

THE EGG SALE BUSINESS

Every homestead has eggs—or at least most do. Some of us get just six eggs a day, others get hundreds. Depending on your space and needs, you can make quite a bit of money off of egg sales. You certainly won't get rich, but you'll make enough to cover the cost of feed (and maybe more), and it opens up an entirely new door to a group of people who may be willing to buy other homestead products from you, like jams, produce, homemade goods, and meat.

The Egg Sale Business

So how do you run a successful egg business? Well, there are some things to consider. You'll first need to do your research on your local market. Some rural areas are already saturated with egg sales, but here are a few ways you can be successful.

Start with the Eggs

Your eggs must be *clean* and *beautiful* if you plan on attracting customers. The average customer who will purchase a dozen eggs for $5 isn't going to be a farmer. It may be someone who is into homesteading and living a more natural life, but they certainly aren't farmers. These customers will want clean and pretty eggs. In fact, I've had people tell me straight to my face that they don't want white eggs because they aren't as "good" as brown and colored eggs. It's crazy, I know, but commercial industries have trained us to think this way. There's not much you can do about the falsities that run amuck, but you can offer quality products to your customers either way. Make sure you're marketing your eggs properly.

TIP

Keep in mind that most states require you to wash and refrigerate your eggs. There is also a limit to the amount of eggs you can sell in certain states before you're required to have a permit. You'll need to do your research before selling.

Your Egg Packaging

Packaging your eggs in fresh, new cartons with labels will help customers feel like they're special. Tie a piece of twine around it with a sprig of rosemary, and you've really got yourself a prize winner! People like to feel they are buying eggs from you because they are getting an impeccable product. Packaging also helps with branding your business.

Here are some things to consider:

The name of your homestead or farm on stamps and labels. This will not only remind your customers about your brand, but also has the potential to lure in new customers.

Brown blank egg cartons. It's always best to use brand-new cartons for each sale, but I do reuse most of my lightly used cartons over and over again.

Mini egg stamps. This stamp is super cute to put on one of the eggs in the center of your carton.

Fresh herbs and twine. Because adding extra love really helps your customers feel special!

Knowing and Choosing Your Egg Market

Who are you going to sell these eggs to now that they are all prettied up? Knowing your market is going to be your best marketing strategy through it all. If you're just selling to friends, family, and a few coworkers, you could probably skip the prettifying stage. However, if you're looking for hard-core customers, you're going to have to travel into the city (or farmers' market) once a week, every other week, or once a month. You can also tag-team city farmers' markets with a friend, or add on to a farmer already going to market and just commission them to sell your eggs for you. You can also check with local (especially rural) stores that might allow you a space to sell eggs.

Here are ways to do exactly that:

Sell eggs to your family, friends, and coworkers. This is just plain common sense. You already see them and spend time with them. They are your first immediate target market.

Understand that your market might include city folk. While your rural friends will buy eggs from you too, especially the Mayberry friends, most of your egg sales will only bring in money if you market to people living a non-rural or non-homesteading lifestyle. This is where the prettifying comes in handy.

Place your eggs on local farm sale websites. Social media, local newspapers, online groups, and forums are all great places to market your eggs.

Tag-team a farmers' market with a friend. Or join up with a farmer who's already going to market. Chances are, they will gladly sell your eggs for you at their table. Barter with eggs or other homestead items in return, or offer to go watch their stand once a month, and you've got yourself a sweet setup.

Once you've found your market and pulled your branding material together, it's time to market yourself! You'll want to make sure your customers know that your hens are fed an all-natural and herbal diet. You'll also want to be in compliance with the current FDA rules for egg sales. For example, you may not be able to say "pasture raised" without a certificate from the government, but you can absolutely say "farm fresh" along with a description of your eggs. Check your state's laws before making any final marketing decisions, however. When in doubt, call your local extension office.

The Meat Bird Business

If you're selling your extra eggs, chances are those same customers will buy processed birds from you. While we aren't going to go over the steps of how to process a meat bird, here are some easy steps you can take in creating and marketing a successful meat bird business.

Choosing Your Meat Breed

There are several different meat breeds to choose from. You'll need to decide what you like for your own table, and then consider what others might like for theirs. You can choose the common hybrid chickens, or you can go with a heritage breed that takes a little longer to raise and is a bit smaller. It's ultimately up to you and your market.

Choosing Your Meat Setup

You'll sell more meat if you set up a pasture-ranging system—pasture-raised meat sells better. Much like Joel Salatin's chicken tractors, you can build your own with free templates found online. Meat birds simply need a place to shelter out of the elements and some feed and clean water, and they are good to go. You can offer a small dust bathing area if you'd like, but there's no guarantee they will use it. Move the system each day for fresh pasture, and don't free-feed them so they're encouraged to range more often.

Homemade Broiler Feed

Making a homemade broiler feed is absolutely attainable. Simply use the homemade layer feed recipe on page 88 and increase the protein rationing by adding more sea kelp, black oil sunflower seeds, cultured dry yeast, or fish meal. If you are pasture-raising your birds, you can give them the same protein layer feed as you do your regular chickens. Pasture-raised birds grow about 3 weeks slower than non-pasture-raised birds.

If you aren't able to pasture-range your meat birds, you can still offer them home-made chicken feed, kitchen scraps, and more. Being able to market them as all-natural as possible will be your greatest selling point, and it will create a healthier bird.

Marketing and Selling Your Processed Chicken

Now that you've processed your birds, it's time to sell them. You'll market them just as you would your eggs—all natural, non-GMO, free-ranged, etc. But once again, before slapping a label on it, check your state laws to see what is acceptable. When in doubt, contact your local extension office.

Here in my state, at the time of writing this book, we're allowed to sell fewer than 1,000 processed birds from our homestead, but that's not the same in every state. Some states require you to process all of your birds in a licensed kitchen. Others allow you to sell directly from your farm. Again, check with your local extension office if you can't find a firm answer.

Once you've figured out your labels and local laws, you can start marketing online, in online forums, in newspapers, and in local groups. Don't forget to market to your egg customers first—they are a great instant customer base for your processed poultry!

Keep in mind that in some states you are not allowed to sell processed meat at farmers' markets unless you have a permit.

And just like that, you can have a successful eggs and meat business! If you can do both of these on your homestead, you'll have an entire chicken business devoted to offering quality food and livestock to your community and beyond. Take pride in your natural chicken keeping practices, and others will as well. It will show in the amount of sales you make and the people you meet. There's one more type of chicken business you can get into, however—the chicken breeding business. Let's go over that next.

CHAPTER

13

THE CHICKEN BREEDING BUSINESS

My favorite chicken business is the one that involves breeding. I get so much joy out of matching pairs and genetics, watching egg colors become deeper and more vibrant, and hatching out lots of baby chicks!

I could write a book entirely about the chicken breeding business, but that's another topic for another day. For now, let's talk about the basics, and how you can make money doing it.

Choosing Your Breeds and Being Cautious

We've raised French Black Copper Marans off and on since first getting chickens. They are a highly sought-after breed, so I knew if I could offer good-quality breeding stock, I could have a successful business while still putting out good genetics into the chicken world. I wanted to raise this breed naturally, but they were fairly expensive to start with. So in order to offset my costs, I needed to sell breeding stock. It was a win-win.

The Marans were great, but it wasn't until we bought quality, rare, Icelandic chickens that I realized the rarity of the breed really did make a difference. Before I even had my breeding stock set up and ready to produce, I had a waiting list of over 150 people wanting to purchase hatching eggs. I knew I would have to educate others that ordering from just anyone doesn't mean you'll get what you pay for. I also knew I'd have to educate others on what the breed standard truly is. Genetics can be so sensitive.

I learned that I shouldn't have taken orders before I knew what my stock would produce. And as a customer of rare breeds, I learned not to jump head first into buying from a breeder without first doing research, asking questions, and requesting pictures of the breeding stock before making a final decision.

Breeding to Standard or for Hobby

You can either breed your chickens to standard or breed for hobby. This may not be the way a professional would explain it, but bear with me. I've been in the chicken breeding world long enough to know what you might run into.

Breeding to Standard

This means that you are breeding to the *Standard of Perfection,* the exact standard of what the American Poultry Association deems true to that breed in terms of coloring, characteristics, depth of egg color, and so on. You can purchase books, and you should, about your specific breed and what their standards are. Most chicken breeds also have their own organizations and clubs, which will help you out a lot when trying to find your own breeding stock.

Those who are breeding to standard want the entire package—the look, the temperament, and the egg size and color.

Breeding for Hobby

This means that you're simply concentrating on one or two things when it comes to your breed. Some people only want to breed Marans because of their dark egg color. For generations of chickens, they might only hatch their darkest eggs, and then have a new generation of even darker egg layers. Hobby breeders aren't breeding for the "entire package" or standard of perfection. While this is completely fine, you'll need to make sure you convey this to your customers. Genetics can get tricky, and if you're breeding for egg color but not a standard physical characteristic (like feathered legs), it could be a disappointment for your customer.

Breeding and Selling Your Stock

Now that you've chosen your breed and how you'd like to breed your chickens, the same all-natural chicken raising rules apply. They will especially apply to birds you want to keep healthy and strong, since you've put a lot of work and money into them. (Make sure you're utilizing Part 3 of this book to ensure optimal health for your breeding stock.) After all, they will be working for you the hardest!

Here are a few ways to sell your breeding stock:

Sell hatching eggs. This is the most common way to purchase breeding stock from a breeder. However, you will need to check your state laws on how many eggs you can sell through the mail, and if any permits or certifications are required. You'll also need to make sure to package the eggs well so that they get to their destination safely and unharmed. You can sell hatching eggs from $1 to $20 per egg, depending on the breed. Don't forget to charge for shipping, as it can cost between $15 and $30 per dozen.

Sell chicks and juvenile birds. Another common way to sell breeding stock, this allows you to hold back chickens and juveniles you might want to keep for yourself and then sell chicks by mail or locally. You can sell chicks for $2 to $25 per chick, depending on the breed. Juvenile birds can be sold for $15 to $50, depending on the breed.

Sell adult birds. There are many people who want to start breeding their birds right away. That's where this option comes in handy for the breeder. Sell off your old stock to make room for new stock, or simply grow out stock so that you know what they are producing, then sell the ones you're not interested in keeping. You can sell adult birds locally for $25 to $100 a bird, depending on the breed and standard.

There are innovative ways to market and sell your stock, but make sure you always let people know that your chickens have been raised naturally. This is a major selling point for potential buyers who want to purchase truly healthy livestock.

Where to Market Breeding Stock

Here's where you can market your breeding stock:

- at your feed store
- with social media groups
- in the local newspaper
- on your website
- at the farmers' market
- through chicken breed standard organizations
- through giveaways
- through egg and chick raffles

Keeping Your Breeding Stock Pure

Last but not least, it's important to make sure that if you're breeding to standard and not a mixed breed, you'll need to keep your stock pure. You can do this one of two ways: by implementing breeding pens so that only one breed is in each pen, or by keeping one flock with your main breed of rooster and hens.

Setting Up Breeding Pens

In his book *The Small-Scale Poultry Flock*, Harvey Ussery talks about his rotational breeding pen setup. In order to keep a distance in relationship between offspring, roosters will need to be rotated each year. You can do this by labeling your pens by color—red, green, and blue—and leg banding your chickens in that group.

The offspring of each color pen stays with the hens of that pen. The only thing that changes is the rooster. So the red rooster moves to the green pen (keeping his red leg band), the green rooster moves to the blue pen (keeping his green leg band), and so on. However, the offspring of that rooster stay within the pen from which they were produced and then labeled the same color as the mothers. This produces diversity in your flock so that chicks aren't closely related.

Running Your Flocks Together

The breeding pen setup can be costly and confusing, so I prefer to run my flocks together. You can do this by choosing two breeds that play off of each other. For example, my main breed is the French Black Copper Marans (FBCM). I make sure the bulk of my flock are FBCM hens and two FBCM roosters. The remainder of my flock is a hodgepodge, but none of them lay dark brown eggs like my FBCM hens do. I know that when I collect my FBCM eggs, they are pure FBCM offspring because I only have FBCM roosters.

I can then add a true blue egg layer, like an Ameraucana, Araucana, or Cream Legbar. When I collect the blue eggs, I know that my offspring will be an Olive Egger because of the genetic mix between the blue egg layer and the FBCM. This allows me to offer two breeds—FBCM and Olive Eggers—to sell as breeding stock, gives me flexibility in playing with egg colors, and more. Just make sure you band your chicks accordingly in case one of your Olive Eggers pops out a dark brown egg one day!

Ultimately, have fun with your breeding program and system, and remember that putting out a good genetic pool is essential to conserving breeds and keeping breeds in their natural genetic state. It's okay to have fun with breeding and to offer breeds for sale, but it's not okay to be a breeder who isn't bettering a breed and is instead simply trying to make money off of the rarity or name of a breed.

6

A Family That Gathers Together

MY SON—THE SPITTING IMAGE OF HIS FATHER with his baby-blue eyes—must've been about 4 years old (going on 40) the day he asked if he could collect the chicken eggs all by himself.

I secretly watched from the back deck as he walked down to the chicken coop, his footsteps firm but shaky with excitement. He was doing a big thing, and this was a moment to be proud of.

There was only one egg in the coop that morning, but you would've thought it were an entire dozen from his squeals of excitement. He carefully walked back up the hill, and we met in the center of the hallway. Smiling widely, he had his hand behind his back, hiding his little prize. "Well, did you find any eggs?" I asked him.

His smile broadened wider than a country mile, and as he pulled his hand from behind his back, the egg flew into the air and splatted on the floor. Tears quickly streamed down my son's face. He had been so careful, and now the egg was ruined.

I giggled and said, "Well, you can't scramble eggs on the floor, goofy!" He grinned a bit, but I could tell his heart was broken.

Later that evening, right before dusk, I grabbed my basket, hoisted this same sweet 4-year-old on my hip, and said, "Let's gather them together this time."

INVOLVING YOUR FAMILY ON THE FARM AND IN THE KITCHEN

Lots of urban farmers and both small- and large-scale homesteaders have chickens on their property nowadays, and many of us have growing families. Whether you raise chickens strictly for sustainability or as pets, involving your family can be a valuable part of chicken keeping. Not only are you gathering together and making time for chores as a family, but you're also teaching a future generation about keeping chickens naturally.

Children are the future of the farming industry, and what an incredible opportunity we have to instill in them the love of organic farming. If the average farmer is 65 years old, who's going to take his place when he's gone?

Not only that, but involving your children will teach them to appreciate growing their own food. They'll learn how to stick to a schedule, how to be responsible, and maybe even start their own business!

Chicken Chores for Children

While it's easier (and so much quicker) to do chores on your own, start your mini chicken keepers off with smaller tasks and then move on to certain chores depending on their age. Here is list broken down by age-appropriate tasks and chores:

1 to 3 years. *With supervision*, children can place eggs in and take them out of baskets. They can also toss treats to the chickens. Up until the age of 4 (and even beyond), children have ultra-sensitive and immature immune systems. They are very susceptible to contracting bacteria. Make sure you're not allowing your littlest chicken keepers to do things that could cause them to place their hands in their mouths and transfer bacteria into their bodies.

4 to 6 years. *With supervision*, children can place eggs in and take them out of baskets, replace nesting box bedding, feed and water chickens (with limitations), and offer treats and entertainment to the flock.

7 to 9 years. At this age, you should start considering individual tasks and chores that your child can do without supervision. Start by giving them the singular task of feeding and watering on their own. This includes rinsing out the waterers each day. While they do these chores, you can monitor them while you're doing other tasks around the chicken area. Once they've mastered one chore without supervision, you can begin adding more, such as seasonal coop cleaning and daily coop freshening.

At this age, children can also begin to learn about administering herbs and doing health checks *with supervision*, and they can also help set up brooders and tend to chicks (again, *with supervision*). This is also a great age to start exploring the local 4-H clubs in your county.

10 or more years. At this age, if your child has been around chickens and is experienced in chicken keeping chores, now is the time they can really flourish with their own chicken chores completely on their own. From 10 years on, children can independently take care of chickens if they have some prior experience. If not, start at the 7 to 9 age and work your way up.

Children can feed and water chickens, clean out waterers and feed bins, carry feed bags, administer herbs (with some super-vision), do routine health checks, fix simple chicken coop and run issues, clean the coop when needed, freshen the coop each day, help tend to and set up chicks (some can do this all on their own), and basically do all of the things that any chicken keeper would do. Use sound judgment on things like wing clipping and spur removal, as they may still need some help with the tougher tasks.

My husband isn't really a poultry person. I knew this from the very beginning of our jour-ney. He tolerates my chicken addiction, and he loves to reap the benefits of fresh eggs each day and chicken manure for the garden. But actually getting up and doing chicken chores? Yeah, no.

My son, on the other hand, is a duck lover. He loves ducks of all ages and will do farm chores like nobody's business when it comes to ducks. But chickens? He only likes chickens at the baby chick through juvenile stage. While he has had his fair share of favorite chickens over the years, I discovered that forcing him to do any type of chore made him not want to do it even more.

Chicken Safety

Chickens can carry bacteria that can transfer to humans. Make sure your mini chicken keepers always wash their hands thoroughly after doing chores or playing with livestock. They espe-cially shouldn't snuggle up with their feathered friends, or give them kisses, as this can transfer nasty bacteria. Likewise, your children can harm your chickens as well! Teach your littles how to handle, hold, and carry chickens before allowing them free-range of the flock.

I've learned to keep it natural not only with my chickens, but with my family as well. The thought of a family gathering and doing chores together is romantic, but the reality is just the opposite. There are kids and other family members who simply have no interest in it. Instead of forcing them into a chore routine, try handing them an opportunity.

People may not realize this, but Joel Salatin, one of the greatest chicken keepers of all time, is quite an encouraging parent and grandparent. In his book *Folks, This Ain't Normal*, he talks about how children aren't born instilled with the desire to do farm chores, but he's encouraged his children and grandchildren by giving them ownership of something.

So, for example, they got their own chicken-mobile to raise their very own chickens, and they were solely responsible for the health and well-being of those animals. The best part, however, is that they got to turn their chores into a business. The children were responsible for finding egg buyers for their chickens. If they preferred breeding the birds, the children had to find buyers for hatching eggs, chicks, and adult chickens.

Turning chores into a business encourages your family members to thrive and flourish in your chicken farming adventure. Not only that, but it's a great character-building technique. It's a *real-life* situation where they get to see the inner workings of a business and the hard work that goes into it. What an incredible way to prepare your children for the real world once they are older!

There are so many other ways that your family can "gather" together, like cooking alongside Mom and Dad. Let's move on to the best part of the gathering—the food!

Farmhouse Egg Recipes

It's the little hands that pull up a chair and the voice that says, "Mama, can I help you cook?" that get me the most. I often have to remind myself to slow down and take joy in the "help" that a child will offer. Involving my child and the entire family in the process of making our food, from start to finish, is a key ingredient to their self-sufficiency in life. I find that more often than not, my son gets just as much joy out of cooking as I do when he knows where his food comes from. And after all, that's the ultimate goal, right?

When you've raised the chicks into egg layers, it is so pleasing to the home-steader and their family. But the magic doesn't actually happen until you're in the kitchen, cooking those eggs and seeing eyes light up. *We grew this, we raised this.*

Some say that the fondest memories you'll ever have are from gathering around the family table, and while I couldn't agree more, sometimes I believe that the fondest memories actually happen *on the way* to the dining table. From the moment you ordered those chicks at your farm store to the satisfaction of cooking your harvest in your kitchen for family or friends, there is no fonder memory, or trail of memories, than this.

My palate is much more sophisticated than the other members in my household, but if there's one thing we can agree on, it's this: Simple, easy egg dishes are one of our favorites. I'd love to share some of our family favorites with you. Not only are they delicious, but they are also full

of some of the very same herbs that you offer your chickens on a regular basis, and herbs that you've learned about throughout this book.

TOMATO, BASIL, AND MOZZARELLA FRITTATA

It sounds like a fancy dish, but there's really nothing fancy about it at all. Much like quiche, but without the crust, this frittata is great to make ahead for breakfast, especially for the gluten-free family member!

3 tablespoons olive oil
½ onion, diced
8 large eggs
½ cup milk or cream
½ teaspoon salt
½ teaspoon pepper
1 medium tomato, sliced
1 handful fresh basil, sliced
Crumbled or sliced mozzarella cheese
½ cup shredded fresh Parmesan cheese

Method:

1. Preheat oven to 350°F.

2. In a cast-iron skillet (or any oven-safe skillet), preheat olive oil over medium heat.

3. Add onion and cook until softened.

4. In a separate bowl, combine eggs, milk, salt, and pepper. Whisk well.

5. Pour egg mixture into hot skillet. Evenly distribute tomato, basil, and mozzarella on top. Sprinkle with Parmesan cheese.

6. Allow mixture to cook on medium heat for about 2 to 3 minutes, or until the edges begin to crisp up, then transfer to your preheated oven and cook for 10 to 15 minutes. Don't overcook. Remove the frittata right when it is cooked through but still a little jiggly. It will continue to cook as it rests.

7. Allow the frittata to rest for 5 minutes before cutting and serving warm.

Some of our favorite variations of this dish:

Tomato, basil, and feta cheese

Zucchini, potato, and feta

Tomato, potato, and jalapeño

Spinach, sausage, and Parmesan

Avocado, chicken, tomato, and feta

Bacon, tomato, and cheddar cheese

HAM AND CHEESE QUICHE

If I'm up to my ears in eggs, I make quiche. There are so many different variations, and the piecrust gives it that extra comfort of "home"... the perfect eggy comfort food!

For the piecrust:
½ pound cold butter
3 cups unbleached all-purpose flour
1 tablespoon apple cider vinegar
⅓ cup cold water
1 egg

Method:

1. With a grater, shred cold butter into flour and toss. Mix with a spoon or your fingers until it creates a sandy texture.

2. Add vinegar, water, and egg and mix well. Do not add more liquid. Simply use your hands to mix the dough until it is completely kneaded and soft.

4. Form the dough into a ball and split in half. Flatten into thick discs and freeze or refrigerate until ready to use. If using immediately, allow the dough to rest in the freezer for about 15 minutes before rolling out.

For the quiche:
3 tablespoons butter (or bacon grease)
½ onion, diced
7 eggs
2 cups heavy cream
1½ teaspoons dill

1 cup diced cooked ham
1 cup shredded cheddar cheese
Salt and pepper to taste
1 premade piecrust (page 199)

Method:

1. Preheat oven to 400°F.

2. In a skillet, melt butter and cook onion until softened. Remove from pan.

3. In a large bowl, beat together eggs and heavy cream until a bit fluffy. Add dill, ham, and cheese. Season with salt and pepper if desired.

4. Add cooked onion to egg mixture and combine well.

5. Pour mixture into piecrust that has been prepared in a tart pan or pie pan.

6. Bake for 45 to 60 minutes or until the center of the quiche isn't jiggly.

7. Allow to cool for 10 minutes before cutting and serving. Serve warm.

Some of our favorite variations of this dish:

Sausage, bacon, and cheddar cheese

Tomato, spinach, and thyme

Tomato, basil, and goat cheese

STEAK, EGG, ARUGULA, AND GOAT CHEESE PIZZA

This recipe is great if you have leftover steak, loin, or roast from a previous dinner. Otherwise, simply cook your meat ahead of time before assembling (as seen in recipe). One of my favorite pizzas of all time, I could eat this any time of day. It really is that good!

Basic Pizza Dough
1 teaspoon active dry yeast
1½ cups warm water
4 cups unbleached all-purpose flour
⅓ cup olive oil

1. Pour yeast and warm water into a bowl. Let sit for 5 minutes.

2. In a separate bowl, mix flour, olive oil, and water and yeast mixture until combined.

3. In a separate large bowl, add just a bit of olive oil to the bowl. Remove dough from previous bowl, flip it a couple of times in the olive oil in the new bowl. Cover with a towel or plastic wrap and allow to rise for 1 hour.

4. Divide in half to make 2 pizza crusts when ready to use. You can freeze the extra crust if you don't need it right away.

Pizza Ingredients
3 tablespoons butter
4 ounces beef loin or roast, sliced
1 cup arugula, chopped
1 ball pizza dough
2 teaspoons thyme
2 teaspoons minced garlic
2 ounces goat cheese, chèvre, or feta
6 eggs
1½ teaspoons sea salt
1 teaspoon pepper
Balsamic vinegar (optional)

Method:

1. Preheat oven to 400°F.

2. In a skillet over medium heat, add 1 tablespoon butter and cook sliced pieces of meat until medium rare (about 1 minute per side). Remove from pan.

3. Add 1 tablespoon butter to skillet and wilt arugula. Remove from pan.

4. On a large rectangle pizza tray or cookie sheet, spread out pizza dough into a rectangle. Bake for 5 minutes, then remove from oven. Brush with 1 tablespoon butter or olive oil. Sprinkle with thyme and garlic.

5. Layer on arugula, steak, and goat cheese pieces.

6. Crack 6 eggs on top of the pizza, leaving about 1 inch or so between each egg. Salt and pepper to taste.

7. Place pizza back in oven and cook for 15 minutes or until crust is golden.

8. Remove pizza from oven and allow to sit for 5 minutes before cutting and serving warm. You can drizzle a little balsamic vinegar over the top of the pizza for extra zing and depth of flavor.

ANN'S PICKLED EGGS

My friend Ann makes the best pickled anything. She is the food preservation queen, and I am so thankful she's always willing to share her recipes. Here's a favorite!

1 dozen large eggs or 2 dozen bantam eggs, steamed and peeled
½ sweet onion, chopped
1 jalapeño pepper, sliced
1 cup white vinegar
1 cup water
1 cup refined sugar
1 teaspoon thyme, dried
2 teaspoons mustard seed

Method:

1. Combine cooked eggs, onion, and jalapeño in a bowl.

2. Add vinegar, water, and sugar to a saucepan and bring to a boil. Add thyme and mustard seeds and bring back to a hard boil. Boil for 5 minutes.

3. Fill jars with steamed eggs and veggies, and add brine until it completely covers the mixture.

4. Cap and allow the jars to sit in the refrigerator for 1 week before opening.

How to Steam Eggs

Steaming your eggs, rather than boiling them, is the only way to quickly and easily remove the shell from your farm-fresh eggs. Steaming them allows the shell to come away from the white of the eggs more easily, allowing the shell to slip right off. Simply steam the eggs in a steamer or steam basket for 10 minutes, remove from heat, drain, and submerge in ice-cold water for several minutes before peeling.

SPICY EGGS AND POTATO SKILLET

When I first started eating a whole-food diet, this was my go-to meal. I had to break the mindset of things I thought I wanted to eat, and actually concentrate on the things I should be eating. I knew that with my new diet, I could eat eggs and potatoes, and from that knowledge this spicy eggs and potato skillet was born. Mix and mingle different ingredients to make it your own! You certainly don't feel like you're on a diet with this dish.

4 tablespoons butter or olive oil
4 potatoes, diced
1 lb sausage
2 banana peppers
1 bell pepper, diced
1 zucchini, diced
3/4 cup cherry tomatoes, cut in half
1/2 sweet onion, diced
1 teaspoon minced garlic
1 tablespoon thyme
Salt and pepper to taste
3–4 eggs
Hot sauce (optional)

Method:

1. In a large skillet brown sausage. Remove from pan, drain, and set aside.

2. In the large skillet you used for sausage, over medium heat, add 2 tablespoons butter or olive oil.

3. Add potatoes and cook until almost completely done.

4. Add remaining 2 tablespoons butter or olive oil. Add banana peppers, bell pepper, zucchini, cherry tomatoes, onion, garlic, thyme, and salt and pepper. Cook until veggies are softened but still crisp. Add eggs and cook until scrambled into your potato hash.

5. Add sausage back to mixture.

6. Drizzle your choice of hot sauce over the entire dish. Serve warm.

BREAKFAST CASSEROLE

This casserole is so incredibly easy and is a staple in our house. If I've had a long day and we just want something healthy and quick, this is the casserole I go for an evening meal. It's just as easy to throw together in the morning! To save even more time, just buy pre-shredded frozen potatoes at the store. Make it your own by adding other seasonings and veggies, like mushrooms and bell peppers, and different types of cheeses. My son and I especially like to add our favorite hot sauce to this dish.

5-6 cups shredded potatoes
1 pound breakfast sausage
1 small yellow onion, diced
6 eggs
½ cup milk
1½ teaspoons garlic powder
Salt and pepper to taste
2 cups shredded cheddar cheese
1 cup shredded gouda cheese

Method:

1. Preheat oven to 425°F.

2. Place shredded potatoes into a buttered casserole dish (9 x 13 or smaller). Place dish in the oven for 10 minutes while preparing the rest of the ingredients.

3. In a skillet, brown the sausage. Add onions and cook for an additional 5 minutes.

4. In a bowl, combine eggs, milk, salt, pepper, and garlic powder. Mix well.

5. Pull potatoes out of the oven and pour egg mixture over the potatoes. Crumble onion and sausage mixture on top of potatoes. Cover the entire dish with a mixture of cheddar and gouda cheese.

6. Cover casserole and cook for an additional 30 minutes. Remove from oven, uncover, and allow to cool for about 5 minutes before serving. Serve warm with scallions, sour cream, or hot sauce!

OLD-FASHIONED CUSTARD PIE

When I think of sweet egg treats, I think of
custard pie, which has probably been around
since the Stone Age (just taking a guess here).
But really, it's a recipe that's been tested by time
and generations of bakers, and it's one of the best
ways to use up a lot of extra eggs when you need
a dessert!

1 piecrust (page 199)
3 eggs
2 cups whole milk
½ cup granulated sugar
1 teaspoon nutmeg
1 teaspoon vanilla

Method:

1. Preheat oven to 350°F. Roll out piecrust into pie pan.

2. With a fork, poke holes in the bottom of your piecrust. Bake crust for 10 minutes or until the crust begins to harden.

3. In a large bowl, whisk together all of the remaining ingredients. Pour the mixture into the prepared piecrust, cover the edges of the crust with aluminum foil, and bake the pie for an additional 20 to 30 minutes, or until a toothpick or knife inserted in the center comes out clean.

4. Allow pie to cool completely before serving. This pie is best if refrigerated for a couple of hours before serving.

HOMESTEAD POUND CAKE

My husband loves pound cake. He asks for it often, and some days I comply, other days I don't. This recipe I finally mastered! Use this simple homestead pound cake recipe as the base for whatever you'd like to add. If you want to make a chocolate pound cake or any other flavored pound cake, omit the lemon zest. The rest of the ingredients stay the same.

1 cup salted butter, softened
1½ cups granulated sugar (or raw evaporated cane juice)
2 teaspoons finely grated lemon zest
Juice of ½ lemon
1½ teaspoons vanilla extract
1½ teaspoons almond extract
5 eggs
2 cups unbleached flour

Method:

1. Preheat oven to 325°F.

2. Flour a loaf or Bundt pan. (Fills one large loaf pan or two small loaf pans) Set aside.

3. In a large bowl, cream together butter and sugar. Beat in lemon zest, lemon juice, vanilla extract, almond extract, and eggs. Combine well.

4. Fold in flour in small batches until it's all well combined. Do not overmix.

5. Pour batter into loaf pans or a Bundt pan. Bake for 45 to 55 minutes, or until a knife or toothpick comes out clean when inserted in the center. If the cake begins to brown too quickly, cover with foil.

6. Allow cake to cool in pan for about 10 minutes, then remove and continue cooling on a wire rack until cooled completely.

For the drizzle (optional):
2 cups powdered sugar
 4-5 teaspoons milk
1 teaspoon vanilla
¼ teaspoon lemon zest, finely grated

Method:

Combine all the ingredients and drizzle over warm pound cake, allowing the glaze to soak in.

OLD-FASHIONED CUSTARD ICE CREAM

Believe it or not, I'm not a huge fan of ice cream unless it's chocolate. However, this custard-based ice cream is one of our favorites. You can switch up the flavors as you like, and it works great in an old-fashioned crank ice cream maker or an electric one!

4–5 egg yolks
½ cup granulated sugar (or evaporated cane juice)
1 cup whole milk
1 cup heavy cream
2½ teaspoons vanilla extract

Method:

1. In a medium saucepan, combine egg yolks and sugar.

2. In another small saucepan, heat the milk until it simmers, then slowly add the milk to the egg mixture and combine well.

3. Stir constantly over medium heat until it reaches 165°F or until it thickens. Immediately remove mixture from the saucepan and place it into a bowl. Cool in the refrigerator or on the counter to room temperature.

4. When the custard is ready, add the heavy cream and vanilla. At this point you can add other things as well if you'd like, such as chocolate, berries, or herbs.

5. Churn in your ice cream maker according to manufacturer's instructions. This recipe works well in a hand-crank maker or an electric one. Each recipe makes 1 quart of ice cream.

At the end of a hard-working day, sitting down and seeing the bounty before you on your family's table is comforting. Even more so, it is liberating when you know that you cared for it, raised it, and cooked it all on your own. Knowing that your chickens live a happy life roaming wild and free, and that you give them all the attention they deserve, is the most beautiful part of raising chickens naturally.

Even greater than this is the notion that you truly can grow your own food—whether it's the herbs in your frittata or the ice cream in the freezer. You'll inspire your family, and your family will inspire others. And before you know it there's an entire ripple effect, and a revolution of people taking control of their heritage and food system begins.

That's why gathering together is important, and one of the most natural ways of the modern chicken keeper. And that's why, if at no other time of the day than evening, we gather together as a family to enjoy and bless the bounty that we've worked so hard for—because we deserve it, and so do the animals that sacrificed their time to be here and share their bounty with us.

AFTERWORD

I often think about what life was like before we had chickens. I can't really imagine life without them, if we're being honest. It would be a little too quiet on our homestead without the rooster crowing and the hen singing her egg song.

What I love most about this entire experience, however, is the chance to be part of something greater. My generation is obsessed with chickens, and while it might be a little trendy nowadays, chickens have opened the floodgates to a more sustainable and simple lifestyle. People who raise backyard chickens are more prone to make healthier life choices, like choosing organic items at the grocery store or taking control of their health care by using herbal remedies and natural resources.

While this entire book talks about how to naturally take care of chickens, sometimes I wonder if chickens make us naturally take care of ourselves. We are now in charge of animals that so many of us thought were reserved only for farmers.

Chickens now dot the yards of city subdivisions and rural acreage alike. There is no right or wrong place to house a chicken in modern society. They've become an appendage to our busy lives, attaching themselves to us as we attach ourselves to the homesteading lifestyle that we so desperately crave, and some of us are already living.

As a natural chicken keeper, you'll feel a sense of worth, as if you've done something better in the world just by raising chickens. Hold on to that, because you *have* done something better.

You've enriched the soil that you walk on. You've raised your family's own food source. You've taught your children how to be good stewards of the earth. And you've raised livestock in a natural and efficient way, against everything big companies tell you that you must do in order to raise healthy chickens.

You walk to the beat of your own drum, and friend, there are plenty of us that walk right alongside you.

The chicken revolution has begun. Let's make it worth being part of by making a difference in *how* we raise our chickens—naturally, herbally, and simply, through every single stage of chicken keeping.

TOOLS AND RESOURCES

You've learned a lot in this book, and you might be wanting a quick and easy reference for tools and resources that we use. Here you'll find exactly that!

Tools We Use

My grandmother's collecting basket

Scissors

Nail trimmers

Shovel

Rake

Power washer

Chicken wire

Hardware cloth (¼-inch mesh)

Nesting pads

Little Giant 3-quart feed scoop

Galvanized trash cans (for feed)

Galvanized chicken waterer

8-quart rubber feed and water pans

Products We Use

Virginia Natural Layer Pellets (non-GMO)

Brinsea incubators

Brinsea brooders

Genesis Hova-Bator incubator

FURTHER LEARNING AND REFERENCES

How the Chicken Conquered the World: www.smithsonianmag.com/history/
how-the-chicken-conquered-the-world-87583657
History of the Chicken: https://extension.psu.edu/history-of-the-chicken
U.S. Chicken Industry History: www.nationalchickencouncil.org/about-the-industry/history
History of Egg Production: www.aeb.org/farmers-and-marketers/history-of-egg-production
Vitamins and Minerals Important to Poultry: www.thepoultrysite.com/articles/1070/
vitamins-and-minerals-important-to-poultry
Fermented Feed for Laying Hens: www.ncbi.nlm.nih.gov/pubmed/19373724
Fodder Production Systems: https://wcroc.cfans.umn.edu/fodder
FDA website: www.fda.gov

Herbal Studies

Thyme (antifungal): www.ncbi.nlm.nih.gov/pubmed/17209812
Oregano (antibacterial): www.ncbi.nlm.nih.gov/pubmed/23484421
Astragalus (immunoregulatory properties): www.ncbi.nlm.nih.gov/pubmed/28826771
Astragalus (avian flu): www.ncbi.nlm.nih.gov/pmc/articles/PMC3729712
Stinging nettle (various benefits): http://www.poultrydvm.com/supplement/stinging-nettle
Garlic (mites): www.ncbi.nlm.nih.gov/pubmed/11092328
Meniran herbs (mycoplasma): https://knepublishing.com/index.php/Kne-Life/article/
download/1106/2867
Pumpkinseeds (antiparasitic): www.ncbi.nlm.nih.gov/pmc/articles/PMC5037735
Wild pepper tree, *Loxostylis alata* (brooder pneumonia): https://bmcvetres.biomedcentral
.com/articles/10.1186/1746-6148-8-210
Use of Plant Extracts to Control Necrotic Enteritis (Rot Gut) in Poultry: www.hindawi
.com/journals/bmri/2016/3278359

Further Education and Reading

The Small-Scale Poultry Flock by Harvey Ussery
The Chicken Health Handbook by Gail Damerow
Storey's Guide to Raising Chickens by Gail Damerow
Free-Range Chicken Gardens by Jessi Bloom
Folks, This Ain't Normal by Joel Salatin
Pastured Poultry Profit$ by Joel Salatin
Your Successful Farm Business by Joel Salatin
The Farm Girl's Guide to Preserving the Harvest by Ann Accetta-Scott

50 Do-It-Yourself Projects for Keeping Chickens by Janet Garman

Backyard Chickens: Beyond the Basics by Pam Freeman

Franklin Institute of Wellness (herbal education): https://franklininstituteofwellness.com

Chicken Resources: Coops, Hatcheries, and More

Your local farm store: *Buy local first and foremost!*

Lehman's Hardware Store: www.lehmans.com

Chicken Coop Company: www.chickencoopcompany.com

Urban Coop Company: www.urbancoopcompany.com

Fluffy Layers (egg-collecting aprons and more): www.fluffylayers.com

Egg Cartons (and more): www.eggcartons.com

Substation Paperie (egg and egg carton stamps): www.etsy.com/shop/SubstationPaperie

My Pet Chicken: www.mypetchicken.com

Meyer Hatchery: www.meyerhatchery.com

Murray McMurray Hatchery: www.mcmurrayhatchery.com

Hoover's Hatchery: www.hoovershatchery.com

Ideal Poultry: www.idealpoultry.com

INDEX

ABOUT THE AUTHOR

Amy Fewell is the author of *The Homesteader's Herbal Companion* and founder of The Fewell Homestead blog and website (thefewellhomestead.com). She's a writer, photographer, and the mastermind behind the annual Homesteaders of America conference. She lives in Rixeyville, Virginia.